CONTENTS

Introduction

Dealing with Domestic Violence is the forty-fourth volume in the **Issues** series. The aim of this series is to offer up-to-date information about important issues in our world.

Dealing with Domestic Violence looks at forms of domestic violence, the current situation in the UK and what can be done to protect women and children who are victims of domestic violence.

The information comes from a wide variety of sources and includes:
Government reports and statistics
Newspaper reports and features
Magazine articles and surveys
Literature from lobby groups
and charitable organisations.

It is hoped that, as you read about the many aspects of the issues explored in this book, you will critically evaluate the information presented. It is important that you decide whether you are being presented with facts or opinions. Does the writer give a biased or an unbiased report? If an opinion is being expressed, do you agree with the writer?

Dealing with Domestic Violence offers a useful starting-point for those who need convenient access to information about the many issues involved. However, it is only a starting-point. At the back of the book is a list of organisations which you may want to contact for further information.

*****

The context of domestic violence

Information from NCH Action for Children

Definition

The term domestic violence is used here, as it is in common usage. There are many different definitions of domestic violence. It is important to note concerns do exist about the term and the extent to which it can trivialise and diminish the abuse that women are suffering and the consequences for their children. Violence can be physical, sexual, psychological or emotional and can involve any combination of these. Women from every class, race, and religion are abused, as are disabled and older women.

Figures from research

Domestic violence is the second most common type of violent crime reported to the police in Britain, comprising more than 25% of all reported crime.[1]

In London alone there were 9,800 domestic violence assaults in 1992.[2]

The British Crime Survey (1992) estimates that there are 530,000 assaults on women by men in the home every year.

It has been suggested that as few as 2% of such offences are ever reported to the police.[3]

In Britain, 48% of all female murders are the result of women being killed by their partners.[4]

In 90% of incidents of domestic violence in families, the children were in the same or the next room when the violence took place. One-third of children witnessing abuse try to protect their mother.[5]

In one in three families where the mother is being abused, at least one child is also being directly abused.[6]

21,000 children are currently living in refuges in England and Wales (1993).[7]

Women who experience domestic violence are, on average, beaten 35 times before they ask for help and then make between 5-12 different contacts in an effort to end the violence.[8]

Domestic violence often escalates in severity and frequency.[9]

'Cycle of abuse' theory

It is a commonly held notion that people who experience violence in families when growing up, will in adulthood either be violent themselves or seek out relationships where they are victims of violence. This view or perspective is referred to as the 'cycle of abuse' theory and has been influential in the understanding of, and interventions with, women suffering domestic violence.

The 'cycle of abuse' theory has been powerful for both the public and professional understanding of violence within families. It is suggested that its appeal has been due to some notion of 'common sense'. Many people believe that 'violence breeds violence'.

The 'cycle of abuse' theory is often used as a rationale for intervening in children's lives to prevent them repeating such violent or abusive behaviour when they grow up, by 'breaking the cycle'. We should be offering support to children because they have difficult and distressing experiences. No study has demonstrated that there is a simple 'cycle'. Human beings all respond differently to their experiences depending on the particular circumstances and what sense they make of events. We all think and make decisions before we act similarly or differently to events that we have witnessed.

What we think often determines how we behave and therefore values, beliefs and understandings are important to examine if we are to develop sensitive responses to those who are more vulnerable than ourselves.

Social and structural impacts on women and children

Poverty and material factors

Domestic violence occurs across all classes and cultures and is a global issue. The difficulties faced by women need to be considered within their social and structural contexts, and material factors that affect women's lives should never be underestimated. Poverty, poor housing and limited financial support are realities in many women's lives that affect their choices and care of children. Dobash and Dobash (1992),[10] who have undertaken extensive research in this area, suggest that the most important factors in women's efforts to leave a violent relationship are their economic and employment status.

Women from upper and middle classes also face barriers and difficulties in acknowledging their experience of domestic violence, due to status and social pressures to maintain a particular impression or view of the family.

Racism

Children's responses to witnessing violence or being harmed in the 'cross fire' vary according to such factors as the child's age, emotional and physical development and role in the family. Black children live in a society where the experience of racism outside the family is an everyday reality. Communities and families often provide safety and security from this violence and oppression, but when violence takes place within the home it further adds to the stress and vulnerability that black children experience.[11]

The impacts of racism and how it affects women and children suffering violence has been documented by Mama (1989).[12] The following myths and realities indicate some of the particular difficulties facing black women and their children:

Myths

- That violence to women occurs more in black families.
- That black men are 'naturally' more violent both physically and sexually.
- That black men are more violent

to women because of their own experience of racist oppression and violence.

- The insidious assumptions that some black African Caribbean women are promiscuous, over-sexed and enjoy violence.
- The assumptions that Asian women are passive recipients of male-dominated religions, conforming to harsh Eastern traditions (which may include wife-beating, maiming and killing).

Realities

The reality that black women have experienced difficulties in gaining support and assistance from legal, welfare and protection agencies such as housing, social services, police and the courts due to institutional racism.

It is difficult for black women to choose to leave familiar, if not supportive networks of family and community.

The role of the police in sometimes colluding with the violence against women through inadequate response to 'domestics'; and the discriminatory way the criminal justice system has often responded to both black women and men.

More recently, there has been a recognition of the particular difficulties of black migrant women who have joined their husbands, and subsequently suffered violence at their hands. The 'one-year rule' in British immigration law means that people who have come to join their spouse must stay within the marriage for at least one year before they can apply to stay permanently. Women are therefore unable to leave a violent marriage within this period. They are not entitled to receive basic welfare benefits, so if they do leave they have no means of support. Research by Southall Black Sisters

found that between January 1994 and July 1995, 755 black and migrant women were threatened with deportation because of marriage breakdown. Of these women, 512 are fleeing domestic violence.

'I have managed to escape with my life from a violent man, yet I face another kind of death if I am returned to Pakistan. Sometimes I despair and feel suicidal'

Naheed's Story: Southall Black Sisters – 'Abolish the One Year Rule Campaign'

Wider forms of discrimination and disadvantage

Women and children are also disadvantaged if they have disabilities, learning difficulties, are older, not heterosexual or are socially isolated. Women who are dependent on partners due to health problems or disabilities are faced with particular difficulties in violent situations, especially where they lack resources and support to address their needs. Women may experience various combinations of these disadvantages. They may be subject to discriminatory myths and stereotypes, which prevent or inhibit them from seeking help, and/or previous experience of agency responses that have been in-appropriate or discriminatory.

References
1 *Violence Against Wives*. Dobash & Dobash, Open Books, 1980.
2 Metropolitan Police service statistics.
3 Dobash & Dobash, supra.
4 *Home Office (1993) Criminal Statistics: England and Wales.* London: HMSO, 1992.
5 Women and children at risk: a feminist perspective on child abuse. Stark & Flitcraft. pp.461-493 *International Journal of Health Services*, 18(1), 1985.
6 *Children of Battered Women*. Jaffe, Wolfe & Wilson, Sage Publications Inc., California, 1990.
7 Women's Aid Federation Annual Survey, 1992-3.
8 *What Support – An Exploratory Study of Council Policy and Practice and Local Support Services in the Area of Domestic Violence within Hammersmith and Fulham*

Council. McGibbon, Coope & Kelly. 1989.

9 Dobash & Dobash (1984) supra.

10 *Women, Violence and Social Change.* Dobash & Dobash, Routledge, 1992.

11 Asian Children and Domestic Violence, Imran, Umme, Farvah, in *Children Living With Domestic Violence: Putting Men's Abuse of Women on the Child Care Agenda.* Mullender & Morley. Whiting & Birch. 1994.

12 *The Hidden Struggle: Statutory and Voluntary Sector Responses to Violence Against Black Women in the Home.* Mama, A. London Race and Housing Research Unit, 1989.

• The above is an extract from *Making a Difference – Working with women and children experiencing domestic violence*, produced by NCH Action for Children, ISBN 0 900984 57 0, priced at £5.00. Telephone 0345 626579 or see page 41 for address details.

Quarter of women face violence in the home

By Celia Hall, Medical Editor

Domestic violence is a big public health problem with one in four women subjected to physical abuse at the hands of her husband or boyfriend during her lifetime, doctors said yesterday.

They advised general practitioners to ask women patients about the possibility of abuse at home 'almost routinely'.

The study by the British Medical Association (BMA) said that only a quarter of all incidents are reported to the police and only 36 per cent of women seek outside help.

But surveys have shown that GPs are likely to be the first people outside family and friends to whom women will disclose the physical and mental abuse they suffer.

Dr Jo Richardson, a London family doctor and the co-author of the report, *Domestic violence: a health issue?*, said: 'Women need to believe they can trust us and we need to be more proactive. It may be a question we should be asking women about almost routinely.

'We know, as general practitioners, that violence exists but the figure 25 per cent will come as a surprise to doctors,' she said.

At the launch of the report in London she said that other surveys showed women responded 'openly and honestly' when asked directly by their family doctors about violence at home.

'There are ways of phrasing the questions to show that doctors are sympathetic and understanding.

'Doctors are sometimes over-sensitive about breaking the patient-doctor relationship. In reality, both women who have experienced domestic violence and those who haven't want to be asked about it.'

Dr Lorraine Radford, a senior lecturer in social policy at the Roehampton Institute, London, and the report's co-author, said that domestic violence counted for half of all violent crimes against women and that every week in Britain two women were killed by their husband or boyfriend.

It was important to offer help early as the violence against women tended to escalate, she said.

Family doctors should be prepared to refer women to support agencies and refuges. But only in exceptional circumstances should doctors consider breaking a woman's confidence and going to the police.

Apart from physical violence, women also experience a whole range

Domestic violence counts for half of all violent crimes against women and that every week in Britain two women were killed by their husband or boyfriend

of other forms of abuse. This included domineering and unreasonable behaviour such as demanding a cooked dinner at 2am; humiliation and false threats of violence.

In addition children in the household were likely to be attacked too. 'There is an overlap between wife and child abuse in between 40 to 75 per cent of cases.'

Dr Radford said that wife abuse is witnessed by children in 90 per cent of the incidents.

Men are subjected to physical abuse by women but the problem is believed to be much smaller. According to the British Crime Survey it accounts for six per cent of all assaults on men.

'The document shows the BMA's decision to take the lead and look at domestic violence as an issue and how the medical profession can take a lead,' Dr Radford said. 'We see this report as the start of the debate rather than the final words.'

Prof Vivienne Nathanson, the head of health policy research for the BMA, said the report had been sent to ministers. The association plans to discuss the issue with the royal colleges and the General Medical Council.

'Despite the impressive efforts of the women's refuge movement in the last two decades, domestic violence remains a huge but largely hidden problem,' she said.

'Even now, in 1998, it can be very difficult for women to escape from a violent partner or ex-partner.'

GPs to monitor home violence

By Jeremy Laurance and Kim Sengupta

Ministers are to support a series of measures to curb domestic violence following research that reveals a shocking number of attacks on pregnant women.

Doctors and hospital staff are to be asked to help detect women suffering beatings after learning that one-third of attacks on women take place for the first time when they are pregnant. Experts believe that jealousy provoked by the prospective arrival of a baby drives men to violence.

The report, *Why mothers die*, will be unveiled by the Health Minister, Baroness Hayman, at a conference today. It details how six expectant women have been murdered and thousands more subjected to violent attacks during a two-year period under review.

The Government will call for a far greater vigilance by medical staff to prevent injuries, and ask hospitals and GPs to include questions about domestic violence for all pregnant women.

Assaults by male partners are now recognised to cause greater harm to mother and child than medical conditions which are routinely screened for in pregnancy. Yet the warning signs are often missed.

'The confidential inquiry into maternal deaths', a regular survey conducted by a team of specialists, says questions about violence should be included when a woman's social history is being taken at her first ante-natal visit. In addition to routine questioning to spot those at risk, it says health authorities and NHS trusts must establish strategies for helping those identified.

The report, to be launched at the Royal College of Obstetricians today, examined 376 deaths from all causes associated with pregnancy between 1994 and 1996 and occurring up to a year after the birth. Of these, 268 were directly linked with pregnancy and occurred within 42 days of birth, the definition of a maternal death.

It also shows that domestic violence occurs across all social classes with one in three women estimated to suffer an assault at some time during their lives. Experts claim that violence worsens during pregnancy, and doubles the risk of miscarriage.

The Government will call for a far greater vigilance by medical staff to prevent injuries

John Friend, a consultant obstetrician in Plymouth and a spokesman for the Royal College of Obstetricians, said: 'The male partner suddenly feels threatened when the woman gets pregnant. He sees a rival in the camp... Domestic violence is a very big problem and carries greater risks for the developing foetus and the mother than many of the conditions we routinely screen for such as pre-eclampsia.'

Another survey carried out into domestic violence and pregnancy, based on a sample of 1,000 expectant women, has discovered serious problems in the process of screening abuse.

The study, by Dr Susan Bewley, director of obstetrics at Guy's and St Thomas' NHS Trust, in south London, and Dr Gill Mezey a consultant in forensic psychiatry at St George's Medical School in London, found that up to 25 per cent of pregnant women could not be questioned about domestic violence because they were accompanied at all interviews by their male partners.

Dr Bewley said: 'As a society we have encouraged greater involvement of men in childcare, and it is now difficult to exclude them. As we can see this may not be a good thing in cases where we have vulnerable women and controlling men. This is a problem which cuts across social and racial classes.'

The six women who died as a result of domestic violence were all murdered by their husbands or male partners and are likely to represent only a fraction of the total. From the few cases that were reported, all too obvious warning signs were present, the report says.

Domestic violence

Common, concealed, criminal. Can you go on ignoring it?

Domestic violence

Domestic violence is physical, sexual or mental abuse which usually happens in the home. Overwhelmingly it is inflicted on women by men – most commonly by husbands, partners or ex's.

Common

Domestic violence is far more common than violence in the street, pub or workplace. It accounts for a quarter of all reported assaults, according to the police, yet it has been estimated that only 2 per cent of attacks on women are ever reported.

Almost half of all homicides of women are killings by partners or ex-partners.

Wales has 43 refuges – 5 in South Glamorgan alone – all run by Women's Aid. These safe houses are nearly always full of women and children escaping violent men. Thousands of women approach Women's Aid for information and refuge each year. No one is ever turned away.

Concealed

Violence against women in the home is the hidden crimewave. It often takes place behind closed doors, and can be covered up by those who do it by threats, intimidation and isolation of the chosen victim.

The abuser is often charming to the outside world, reserving his brutality for the secrecy of the home. Many women suffer in silence because they fear no one will believe them.

They may also not leave or call the police because they still love the man, but hate the violence, wanting to believe his promises to stop. Women also keep the secret out of simple terror for themselves and their children, and fear of poverty and homelessness if they leave.

Mental abuse – which can include humiliation, continual criticism, emotional blackmail, deprivation of sleep and contact with friends and family – is the best kept secret of all, because of the lack of visible injuries. It can be the worst sort of abuse, and often accompanies violence.

Criminal

Like anyone else who commits a violent assault, a domestic abuser is a criminal and can be brought to court, charged and sentenced to prison or other penalties.

He can also be ordered out of the house by a judge and told not to return or harass the woman on pain of arrest.

The police and courts now take domestic violence more seriously than ever before. The South Wales force has guidelines for dealing with domestic violence and special units staffed by trained officers. Police now work closely with Women's Aid to improve women's safety and access to legal remedies.

But the scandal is that so few cases ever reach the police or courts.

Can you go on ignoring it?

This campaign (No Excuses) is the first of its kind in Wales, and is aimed squarely at lifting the lid on the hidden scandal of domestic violence.

It challenges the assumptions and illusions many of us have which make it so easy for abusers to get away with the behaviour and so hard for women to come forward to get help.

If you want to know more:

Look out for all the other material the campaign will be producing. Contact the Equal Opportunity Unit of South Glamorgan County Council at County Hall on Cardiff 01222 872610 for further information.

Speak up if you hear men (or women) retelling any of the myths that surround domestic violence (e.g. 'She must enjoy it', 'She was asking for it'). Talk about the issue with your friends and family.

Help your nearest Women's Aid refuge group by raising money for them and supporting their projects. Women are always welcome to apply to become volunteers.

Take action in your workplace or through your trade union – does your employer have a domestic violence policy to help women workers who have been abused?

If you are living in fear of abuse or the memory of it, remember, you are not alone. You don't have to put up with it. You have a right to a life free of violence. There are people who can help you.

Women's Aid offers information on legal, housing, and benefit issues and experienced, confidential and sympathetic help in talking things through, as well as a safe place to stay.

In an emergency you can ring the police (dial 999) – you have the same right to protection from violence as anyone else. The South Wales Police have Domestic Violence Units with trained officers to help you.

For help and advice ring Women's Aid: Cardiff 01222 471020 or 01222 343154 (Ethnic Minority Women).

Vale of Glamorgan 01446 737 330

For leaflets and information on groups elsewhere in Wales and the UK you can ring Welsh Women's Aid on: 01222 390 874.

Police: In emergency dial 999.

Family Support Unit (Advice line) 01222 521 212.

Domestic violence – the myths

If you need to leave home due to physical, emotional or sexual abuse, or just want to talk to someone about your experiences, Women's Aid can help you

The myths . . .

There are many popular myths and prejudices about domestic violence. Not only do these myths lead to many women feeling unable to seek or unworthy of seeking help, but they can cause unnecessary suffering. Women may come to believe the myths in an attempt to justify, minimise or deny the violence they are experiencing. Acknowledging the myths can be an important part of coming to terms with what is really happening to her.

Myth: 'It's just the odd domestic tiff. All couples have them.'
Fact: Violence by a man against the woman he lives with commonly includes rape, punching or hitting her, pulling her hair out, threatening her with a gun or a knife or even attempting to kill her. Often women who have been abused will say that the violence is not the worst of their experiences – it's the emotional abuse that goes with it.

Emotional abuse can include controlling the woman, possibly depriving her of money, clothes, food or sleep. He may try to isolate her from her friends, family and support networks, not letting her use the telephone, or may even lock her in her home. Constant criticism is common – constantly telling her she is ugly, stupid or useless.

Between one and two women are killed by their violent partners or an ex-partner in England and Wales every week.

There is no place for physical, sexual or emotional abuse in a healthy relationship.

'The physical harm, although awful, was often over in minutes – but the mental and emotional abuse never went away – it was there, 24 hours a day.'

Myth: 'She's not really threatened by violence, it's just an excuse to get re-housed.'
Fact: Common sense dictates that most women are not that desperate to live in a crowded refuge or bed and breakfast hotel with their children. Most will have left a perfectly good family home in order to get away from their violent partner. There is also no guarantee that they will find anywhere permanent to live, especially if they do not have any children.

Myth: 'It can't be that bad or she'd leave.'
Fact: Women stay in violent relationships for reasons ranging from love to terror. There are also practical reasons why women stay; they may be afraid of the repercussions if they attempt to leave, they may be afraid of becoming homeless, they may worry about losing their children. They may fear poverty and isolation.

Some women who have experienced domestic violence don't have the confidence to leave. They may be frightened of being alone, particularly if their partner has isolated them from friends and family. It can be very tempting to return to him. She might decide to go back, because the children are really missing their dad, or because she is frightened and insecure and is not getting enough support. Some women believe that their partners will change and that everything will be fine when they go home.

'The kids were really missing their dad, they didn't understand why we had to leave, we had no money, we're living in a lousy bed and breakfast, so we went home to try again.'

Myth: Domestic violence only happens in working-class families.'
Fact: Anyone can be abused. Domestic violence is not confined to working-class or so-called problem families. It happens in urban and rural communities, in high-rise estates and middle-class suburbs, in white and in ethnic-minority families. Any woman can be abused, regardless of her age. She might be any of the women you have come into contact with: your sister, your daughter, your mother, your friend, your colleague, your neighbour.

Domestic violence crosses all boundaries, social and economic, professional, religious and cultural.

Myth: 'They must come from violent backgrounds.'

Fact: Many men who are violent towards their families or their partner come from families with no history of violence. Many families in which violence occurs do not produce violent men. The family is not the only formative influence on behaviour. Blaming violence on men's own experience can offer men who abuse an excuse for their own behaviour, but it denies the experiences of the majority of individual survivors of abuse who do not go on to abuse others.

A violent man is responsible for his own actions and has a choice in how he behaves.

'It's not really his fault – his father used to beat him.'

Myth: 'She must ask for it/deserves it/provokes it.'

Fact: No one 'deserves' being beaten or emotionally tortured, least of all by someone who says they love you. Often prolonged exposure to violence has the effect of making the woman believe that she deserves to be hurt. It distorts your confidence and some women may start to rationalise their partner's behaviour. Often, the only provocation has been that she has simply asked for money for food, or not had a meal ready on time, or been on the telephone too long.

Women often blame themselves because they have been consistently told that the violence is all their fault.

There is no justification for violence.

'I went off sex, after the kids, I was often too tired – but he didn't understand. I can't really blame him for raping me.'

'He said I was a lousy house-keeper, not at all like his mother.'

Where to go for help

If you think you are experiencing domestic violence, would like to talk about it or would like help with finding somewhere safe to stay contact the Women's Aid National Helpline on 0345 023 468.

You can also contact you local Women's Aid group via the telephone directory, your local police station, emergency social services, the Citizen's Advice Bureau, the Samaritans or your local housing department.

Domestic violence – facts

Information from the Women's Aid Federation of England (WAFE)

- Almost half (44%) of all incidents reported by women to the British Crime Survey were domestic violence incidents (British Crime Survey 1996, Home Office).
- Since 1981, the largest increase in violent crimes has been in incidents of domestic violence (British Crime Survey 1996, Home Office).
- A number of local surveys in the UK show between 1 in 3 and 1 in 4 women report having suffered domestic violence at some time in their adult lives.
- A household survey of 430 women in a London borough found that 1 in 3 women had experienced domestic violence at some time in their lives, 12% had been victims of domestic violence in the past year (Jayne Mooney (1993) *The Hidden Figure: Domestic Violence in North London*, Middlesex University Centre for Criminology).
- A survey of 484 women in Surrey's shopping centres found that 1 in 4 defined themselves as having suffered domestic violence from a male partner or ex-partner

since the age of 18 years (Nicola Dominy & Lorraine Radford (1996) *Domestic Violence in Surrey: Towards an Effective Inter-Agency Response*, Surrey Social Services/Roehampton Institute).

- A survey of 281 women attending GP surgeries in West London found that 1 in 3 (33%) reported suffering abuse from a male partner (Alison McGibbon, Libby Cooper & Liz Kelly (1988) *What Support?*, Child and Woman Abuse Study Unit, University of North London).
- A recent survey of 129 women attending GP surgeries in North London found 1 in 9 reported experiences of domestic violence

---

Each year, 45% of female homicide victims are killed by present or former male partners compared to 8% of male victims

---

serious enough to require medical attention in the last 12 months (Elizabeth Stanko, Debbie Crisp, Chris Hale and Hebe Lucraft (1997) *Counting the Costs: Estimating the Impact of Domestic Violence in the London Borough of Hackney*, Swindon: Crime Concern).

- Similar findings are reported from research overseas. For example the largest recent survey of violence against women involved a telephone survey of over 11,000 women in Canada. One in three reported violence from their partners (Statistics Canada (1996) *Survey on Violence Against Women in Canada*).
- A survey of 1000 women in city centres in North England found that 1 in 8 women reported having been raped by their husbands or partners (Painter, K. (1991) *Wife Rape and The Law Survey Report: Key Findings and Recommendations*, Department of Social Policy & Social Work, University of Manchester).
- As many as 1 in 3 marriages that end in divorce involve domestic

violence (Borkowski, Murch & Walker (1983) *Marital Violence*, Tavistock).

- Each year, 45% of female homicide victims are killed by present or former male partners compared to 8% of male victims. On average, 2 women per week are killed in England and Wales by their partners/ex-partners (Criminal Statistics (1992) Home Office).

- Repeat victimisation is common. Half of all victims of domestic violence are involved in incidents more than once (British Crime Survey 1996, Home Office).

- Weapons are less likely to be used in assaults but victims of domestic violence are more likely to be injured (British Crime Survey 1996, Home Office).

- 1 in 4 incidents result in substantial physical injuries. 10% of 129 women surveyed in North London GP surgeries reported being knocked unconscious by their partners. 5% had sustained broken bones as a result of domestic violence (Elizabeth Stanko, Debbie Crisp, Chris Hale and Hebe Lucraft (1997) *Counting the Costs: Estimating The Impact of Domestic Violence in the London Borough of Hackney*, Swindon: Crime Concern).

- Women who are physically abused report physical injuries in on average 4 occasions during a twelve-month period (Jayne Mooney (1993) *The Hidden Figure: Domestic Violence in North London*, Middx University Centre for Criminology).

- 60% of 127 women resident in refuges in Northern Ireland experienced violence during pregnancy. 13% lost their babies as a result (Monica McWilliams & Joan McKiernan (1993) *Bringing it out into the open*, Belfast HMSO).

- Domestic violence often continues and may escalate in severity after separation. As many as one-third of women who leave refuges experience continued abuse and harassment from their ex-partners (Binney, Harkell & Nixon, (1988) *Leaving Violent Men*, Bristol: WAFE).

- Women are at greatest risk of homicide at the point of separation or after leaving a violent partner (Daly & Wilson (1988) *Homicide*, Aldane Gruyter).

- Domestic violence is the least likely violent crime to be reported to the police. Only one out of three crimes resulting in injury are reported (British Crime Survey, 1996).

- Women who suffer domestic violence are likely to underreport incidents of abuse. In a study of 484 women's experiences of violence in Surrey, 2 out of 3 women who defined themselves as victims of domestic violence said they had not told family, friends or agencies about the abuse. (Dominy & Radford (1996) *Domestic Violence in Surrey*, Surrey Social Services/ Roehampton Institute).

- 5% of health years of life are lost world-wide by women because of domestic violence (Social Services Inspectorate, 1996).

- Psychologists in the USA have found parallels between the effects of domestic violence on women and the impact of torture and imprisonment on hostages (Graham, P. Rawlings E. & Rimini, W. (1988) 'Survivors of Terror: Battered Women, Hostages and the Stockholm Syndrome' in K. Yilo & M. Bograd (eds) *Feminist Perspectives on Wife Abuse*, London, Sage).

- Research has shown that these effects include low self-esteem, dependence upon the perpetrator, feelings of hopelessness about ending the violence, a tendency to minimise or deny the violence (Kirkwood, C. (1993) *Leaving Abusive Partners*, London: Sage).

- Victims of marital rape suffer many of the same reactions as other victims of rape, including very severe depression and suicidal tendencies. Feelings of shame and degradation prevent women from talking about this form of abuse (Council on Scientific Affairs, American Medical Association (1992) Physicians and Domestic Violence: Ethical Considerations in

Journal of American Medical Assoc., 267: 3190-3).

- Domestic violence is a factor in 1 in 4 suicide attempts by women (Stark, E. Flitcraft, A. & Frazier, W. (1979) Medicine And Patriarchal Violence: The Social Construction of a 'Private' Event, *International Journal of Health Services*, 9 (3) pp. 461-93).

Children and domestic violence

- A survey of child abuse hospital records in the USA found that 45% of the mothers of abused children were also victims of domestic violence (Stark & Flitcraft, 1988).

- Bowker's study of over 1,000 women living in refuges found that 70% of the women with children said their partners had also been physically violent to the children (Bowker, 1988).

- Other studies reviewed by Hughes et al (1989) have found child abuse and woman abuse occurring together in 40-60% of cases.

- 1 in 3 child protection cases show a history of domestic violence to the mother (Hester & Pearson, 1998).

- Research sponsored by the National Children's Home in the UK found that in 25% of cases the male partner had also been violent to the children (NCH, 1994).

- In 90% of incidents involving domestic violence, the children are in the same or next room (Hughes, 1992).

- The NCH study found 75% of mothers said their children had witnessed domestic violence, 33% had seen their mothers beaten up, 10% had witnessed sexual violence (NCH, 1994).

- Children's responses to witnessing domestic violence vary according to a multitude of factors, including age, race, class, sex, stage of development, role in the family, relationship with parent(s), and the availability of sources of support outside the immediate family situation (Saunders, 1995).

- Children of all ages most often take some form of passive or active support to protect their mothers when witnessing domestic violence (Hester & Radford, 1996).

- Children of all ages phone the police for assistance and a number of research studies suggest that women often attribute their eventual escape to the emotional and practical support provided by their children (Hoff, 1990).

- Girls, in particular, seek to protect younger siblings during violent episodes and offer support or reassurance in the aftermath of violent behaviour (Jaffe et al, 1990).

- When they have contact with fathers after separation, children may take on even greater responsibility to protect their mothers or siblings from violence or neglect (Hester & Radford, 1996).

- Children sometimes feel guilty if they do not come to the aid of their mother. This 'guilt' is often accompanied by self-blame and feelings that they have in some way 'caused' their father to be violent (Saunders, 1995).

- Children may also feel angry towards their mother for not protecting herself or the children, as well as blaming her for causing the violence. Others may be so concerned about their mother's distress that they keep private their own grief (Saunders, 1995).

- More observable behavioural effects include: disobedience, destructiveness in younger boys (Wolfe et al, 1985); nervous, withdrawn and anxious demeanour in younger girls (Hughes, 1986); more difficult temperaments and more aggressive behaviour in both sexes (Holden and Ritchie, 1991); children running away from home (Jaffe et al, 1990).

- Children of battered women will not necessarily grow up to be batterers or victims of domestic violence themselves. No conclusive evidence exists to support the 'intergenerational transmission of violence' thesis or to show that there is a 'cycle of violence' (Mullender & Morley, 1994).

References

Bowker, L. Arbitell, M. & McFerron, J. (1988) 'On The Relationship Between Wife Beating And Child Abuse' in K. Yilo & M. Bograd (eds) *Feminist Perspectives On Wife Abuse*, London: Sage.

Burge, S. (1989) 'Violence Against Women As a Health Care Issue', *Family Medicine*, 21: 368-373.

Hanmer, J. (1989) 'Women and Policing in Britain' in Hanmer, J. Radford, J. & Stanko, E. (eds) *Women, Policing and Male Violence*, London: Routledge.

Hester, M. & Radford, L. (1996) *Domestic Violence and Child Contact Arrangements in England and Denmark*, Bristol: The Policy Press.

Hester, Marianne & Pearson, Chris (1998 June) *Preventing Child Abuse: Monitoring Domestic Violence*, Bristol: The Policy Press.

Hoff, L. (1990) *Battered Women As Survivors*, London: Routledge.

Holden, G. & Ritchie, K. (1991) 'Linking extreme marital discord, child rearing and child behaviour problems: Evidence from battered women', *Child Development*, 62 (2) April 311-327.

Hughes, H. (1986) 'Research with children in shelters: Implications for clinical services', *Children Today*, 21-25.

Hughes, H. (1992) 'Impact of Spouse Abuse On Children Of Battered Women' *Violence Update*, August 1, pp. 9-11.

Hughes, H. Parkinson, D. & Vargo, M. (1989) 'Witnessing Spouse Abuse And Experiencing Physical Abuse: A "Double Whammy"?', *Journal of Family Violence*, 4 (2), pp. 197-209.

Jaffe, P. Wolfe, D & Wilson, S., (1990) *Children of Battered Women*, London: Sage.

Langley, P. (1991) 'Family Violence: Towards A Family Oriented Public Policy', *Families in Society*, 73, 574-6.

McGibbon, A. Cooper, L. & Kelly, L. (1988) *What Support?*, London: Hammersmith & Fulham Council/ Polytechnic of North London.

Mullender, A. & Morley, R. (1994) (eds) *Children Living Through Domestic Violence: Putting Men's Abuse of Women on the Child Care Agenda*, London: Whiting & Birch.

NCH Action for Children (1994) *The Hidden Victims: Children and Domestic Violence*, London: NCH Action for Children.

Saunders, A. (1995) *It Hurts Me Too*, London: Childline/Women's Aid Federation of England/National Institute for Social Work.

Stark, E. Flitcraft, A. & Frazier, W. (1979) 'Medicine And Patriarchal Violence: The Social Construction of A "Private Event"', *International Journal of Health Services*, 9 (3) pp. 461-93.

Walker, L. (1985) *The Battered Woman Syndrome*, New York: Springer Press.

Wolfe, D. Jaffe, P. Wilson, S. & Zak, L. (1985) 'Children of battered women: The relation of child behaviour to family violence and maternal stress', *Journal of Consulting and Clinical Psychology*, 53, 657-665.

- By Lorraine Radford, (Roehampton Institute), Marianne Hester and Chris Pearson (School for Policy Studies, University of Bristol) May 1998.

Why do we love men who beat us?

By Angela Lambert, who was attacked three times by a man she loved

Women who suffer wife-beating call it the invisible crime. It happens behind closed doors, and when it's exposed people are usually astonished.

'But he's such a charmer,' they say of the abusive man. 'How is it possible?'

Yesterday the wife of Shaun Scott, who stars in *The Bill* as Detective Inspector Chris Deakin, described being beaten up so savagely by her husband that he split her cheek and gave her an appalling black eye.

Yet poor Caroline Scott feels it's her fault. She thinks she has failed, that she must have neglected their marriage. She felt she deserved to be beaten. And yes, of course, she is willing to have him back.

Far from being unusual, she is typical of battered wives. They are all too ready to make excuses for the man who knocked them half-unconscious, and they resolve to be a better spouse in future.

Why do wives – and society – show such extraordinary forgiveness towards men such as Shaun Scott?

Wife-beating, like alcoholism, is no respecter of social status. I knew a judge and a senior diplomat who beat up their wives – not to mention a university professor, a top Army officer and a headmaster. All of them pillars of society; all secret wife-beaters.

According to experts in domestic abuse, wife-beaters are often very charming and very plausible. They have to be. Their reputation depends on keeping their violent tendencies secret.

Few people look beneath the surface, and too many find it hard to believe that an apparently sympathetic, gentle, attentive man – let alone a well-spoken, middle-class professional – could be a Jekyll and Hyde figure.

When they're not brutally attacking their partners – sometimes their children – these men can make thrilling husbands and lovers.

I should know; I was once involved with one. He was tender, adoring, passionate.

He promised to be my lifelong soulmate. He would never leave me, never be unfaithful – or so he said. And I believed him. The first time he hit me, my reaction was sheer disbelief.

His agonised guilt and contrition afterwards convinced me that it had been a one-off. Just like Caroline Scott.

I told myself he was under stress at work. After all, he had been complaining of headaches and sleeplessness and, over the previous few weeks, had seemed tense.

I told myself it was my fault for basking in his adoration and not giving enough back.

The second time I was less forgiving. Even though he told me on bended knees, sobbing with shame and self-disgust, that it would never happen again, I had my doubts. I told him that if he hit me a third time, we were finished.

More than a year passed peacefully. Then one night, out of the blue, his rage erupted and he beat me savagely. I had no idea that hard hands and scalding water could hurt so much.

I was left bruised, burned and shocked – but determined. I rang my solicitor and took out an injunction to prevent him coming near me again.

Ironically, I was heartbroken at losing him but I knew that, having attacked me three times, he wasn't likely to stop, no matter what he promised. I was right and I was lucky; I got out.

Yet, like many women, I did not consider myself the 'victim type'. I had a degree, a well-paid job, I owned my house. I was a feminist, a thoroughly liberated woman. All the same, it happened to me.

When the truth about abusive men emerges, people always ask: 'Why on earth did she stay with him?' Most women give the same answer as Caroline Scott: 'Because I still love him.'

The second reason, for women who have children, is that they want to hold the family together. The

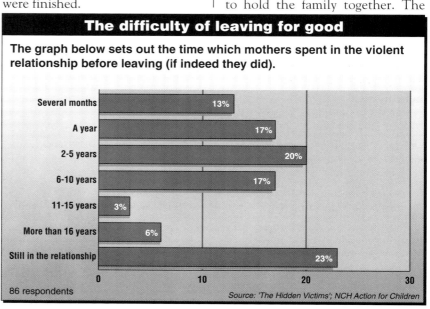

The difficulty of leaving for good

The graph below sets out the time which mothers spent in the violent relationship before leaving (if indeed they did).

- Several months: 13%
- A year: 17%
- 2-5 years: 20%
- 6-10 years: 17%
- 11-15 years: 3%
- More than 16 years: 6%
- Still in the relationship: 23%

86 respondents

Source: 'The Hidden Victims'; NCH Action for Children

children love their father, unless he's a complete lout, and want their parents to stay together.

Many abused wives fear the break-up of the family and its damaging effects on their children more than they fear the brutal blows.

'After all,' they say, 'most of the time he isn't violent. And he's a wonderful dad.'

Many women defend their abuser by claiming that he can't help himself. They liken it to drinking.

An alcoholic will say and do things that wouldn't be possible if he were sober. Most wives with an alcoholic partner hope that, one day, he'll reform.

Besides, it gives them a certain level of power, to be the only one who understands the man's weakness so intimately.

Erin Pizzey, Chiswick Women's Refuge's first director, believed there was another reason why women stayed with the men who battered them: the relationship brought melodrama and excitement to their lives.

A violent marriage is never boring or predictable, while reconciliation can be thrilling and is often sexually passionate.

Abused wives, she concluded, sometimes became addicted to the adrenaline of living on a knife-edge.

One wife said to her: 'After the intensity and passion of that sort of relationship, a peaceful life seems flat by comparison.' Pizzey concluded that many women secretly relished the power they had over their man. An abuser may have physical control over her, but she too has a kind of control because she knows his secret.

This is why the batterer has to grovel afterwards: he needs her co-operation to protect him from public disapproval. Charmers are charming because they want to be liked, and no one likes a wife-beater.

Society is faced with an impossible choice. Should an abusive husband be sent for trial and, if convicted, go to prison?

If so, the consequence is likely to be a one-parent family relying on welfare, and unhappy children who miss their father.

Many such cases lead to divorce, and what happens then? Why, the charmer finds a new wife and the abuse starts all over again.

Research proves that violence is often inherited. We have all come

across families where generation after generation shows a tendency to ungovernable rages, as though the poison were passed through the genes.

Is it realistic to hope it can ever be eradicated?

Of course, if counselling and therapy can help abusers to reform, this is the best possible outcome.

But women can help, too, by remembering it is not their fault.

No woman should tolerate the pain and humiliation of violence, or conspire with their abuser to keep their guilty secret.

If women ceased to suffer in silence, gradually but inexorably, domestic abuse would be despised and outlawed by society, just as child abuse has been in the past 20 years.

Why do men beat women? Because they can. It is high time we expressed our unanimous loathing and contempt for the cowards who beat up those weaker than themselves.

Only then shall we ensure that, in future, they can't.

© *The Daily Mail*
January, 1998

Lucy's story

1985

The first time I saw James I felt certain he was the one for me. I'd just completed my degree and returned from my travels when we were introduced to each other. I was happy and confident. He thought I was gorgeous and I fell in love immediately.

One day we had an upset over something petty and he called me the most horrible things. I couldn't believe it. Coming from a very loving family I had never heard such things before.

Afterwards he was so sorry and took me away to some romantic hideaway for the weekend. I couldn't help but forgive him.

Gradually he became more possessive, especially after I had the children. When I lost my job, he

begged me to stay at home – he could keep me, it would give me the chance to relax. Foolishly I agreed. After that my personality began to gradually slip away as he became more spiteful and cruel.

He never laid a finger on me, he didn't have to. But he started having affairs, would taunt me with them. Once we started making love and he just stopped half-way through and said he was thinking of someone else. He made me feel like nothing.

I kept wanting to leave, but had lost touch with my friends and family. James was the only person in my life and he made me feel so worthless, ugly and depressed. I felt I was a useless wife, a useless mother, a useless lover. There were some good times and then I would try and block out

what he'd done. I'd tell myself he loved me and the children really. But of course it never lasted.

Eventually I attempted suicide and was put in touch with Refuge. A friend had seen their number in some magazine. The woman I spoke to was so kind. She never forced me to leave, but she made me see the abuse wasn't my fault. When I look back now to how I was, I can't believe it. I lost five years of my life somewhere. I still don't fully understand what happened.

But I have two lovely children and that's what matters. For years afterwards, James kept contacting me, begging me to go back, telling me he loved me. Thank God I had the strength to stay away.

© *Refuge*

Violent husbands face a ban from seeing the children

By Steve Doughty, Social Affairs Correspondent

Bullying husbands could be banned from seeing their children in a shake-up of the way the courts deal with broken families.

Government advisers yesterday recommended the measure as part of a sweeping series of powers to help investigate allegations of domestic abuse made by separated wives.

Their report said the proposal which would affect thousands of families, covers 'psychological harassment and subtle emotional abuse' as well as physical violence.

Until now, judges have been urged that it is in the best interests of children that they should continue to see both parents after divorce or separation.

But experts on the Lord Chancellor's influential Advisory Board on Family Law have reversed that guidance because it failed to deal with domestic violence.

Courts had previously 'given the impression that they either condoned domestic violence or did not see it as important', they said.

The board declared: 'That impression needs to be dispelled and mothers need to be reassured that domestic violence will be given proper weight and that the courts will do their best to protect them and their children from it.' According to the advisers, judges needed to 'punish severely any man found guilty of serious domestic violence'.

They stressed: 'Domestic violence does not have to be physical or to result from a lack of impulse control. It can be psychological.

'It includes intimidation and harassment, in both their physical and psychological forms. It may be subtle emotional abuse of the other parent or children.'

The board's radical changes would be made without legislation or debate in Parliament. Under the 1989 Children Act, courts could take on the new powers by accepting updated guidelines.

These can be laid down by a senior judge in a 'practice direction' to the courts or through a judgement in the Court of Appeal. Fathers' groups reacted to the recommendations with alarm. John Campion, of Family and Youth Concern, said last night: 'This is profoundly depressing – a stitch-up.

'To deprive a father of his children is about the cruellest thing you can do. That is a lifelong abuse. 'All the research shows the great

> *The board said courts should consider banning a father from his children even while an inquiry is being made into claims of violence*

majority of violence against children is carried out by the new boyfriends of the mothers or stepfathers.'

Dr Campion added: 'There would not be any serious investigation. The allegation would just lead to fathers being excluded.' Critics are particularly concerned that mothers' allegations of domestic violence would be investigated by court welfare officers.

The 650 or so welfare staff, who are all recruited from probation officers, have long been accused by fathers' pressure groups of bias in favour of women.

Two years ago, the welfare officers' union told members their duty was to 'challenge the experience of oppression of all women in separating families'.

The board said courts should consider banning a father from his children even while an inquiry is being made into claims of violence. Judges would also take account of the level of contrition shown by accused fathers.

Home Office research has suggested one person in 20 suffers domestic violence from a partner,

Factors which persuaded mothers to finally leave their violent partners

Almost nine-tenths (86%) of the mothers for whom there had been a 'last straw' said that they had finally decided to leave because they realised that their violent partner was not going to change.

Factor	%
Realised that he would never change	86%
Afraid that he might kill her	68%
Worried about the effect on the children of witnessing the violence	66%
Afraid that the children would be taken into care	49%
He began hitting the children	23%
He threatened to harm the children	15%

65 respondents

Source: 'The Hidden Victims', NCH Action for Children

with victims numbering as many men as women.

Home Office Minister Paul Boateng has demanded 'a basic shift in attitude' to deal with the issue. But critics say the problem is exaggerated because violence is defined as including minor assaults, such as pushing and shoving, and mental abuse.

Yesterday's report was prepared by a team including lawyers and probation officers, led by family division judge Mr Justice Wall.

Although the board accepted men could be victims, it said women suffered most.

The report refers throughout to violent men and female victims.

At last, help for women living in fear

By Ann Treneman

The Government launched a campaign yesterday to tackle the huge, mostly hidden problem of violence against women. It is the first drive of its kind from any British government, despite the extent of the problem. One woman in four will be attacked in her home at some point and every week two women are killed, by men who supposedly love them.

'We must stop seeing domestic violence as a family secret and see it as something that the whole nation has to focus on,' said Baroness Jay of Paddington, the Minister for Women. She said a battered woman who calls her local authority for help can be passed on to as many as 10 different agencies. 'We must change that,' she said, though authorities will be given five years to do so.

Some £6m will be given over the next two to three years to projects to reduce such violence or help victims. Victim Support will have its grant increased by £6.3m and there is a proposal, though no firm commitment, to a 24-hour helpline. Paul Boateng, the Home Office minister who attended the launch, said there was much to be done in terms of words and deeds. The legal definition of rape, trapped for so long in the 19th century, is in the process of being modernised.

The number of reported rapes in England and Wales has increased by 165 per cent over the past decade – the steepest rise of any crime – but the conviction rate has dropped over the same period from 24 per cent to 9 per cent.

Young men and their attitudes were alarming, he said, drawing attention to a survey that found that one in six young men would force a woman to have sex if she were his wife. 'This is a very real cause for concern,' Mr Boateng said.

The campaign, called Living Without Fear and backed by a 75-page document, it the work of the Women's Unit and the Home Office. It was launched yesterday at a press conference that began at the Cabinet Office but then continued al fresco in St James's Park.

> 'We must stop seeing domestic violence as a family secret and see it as something that the whole nation has to focus on'

There Lady Jay joined two other women: Sally Whittaker who plays a victim of domestic violence in Coronation Street, and Karen Newman, from Norfolk, whose brother-in-law stabbed her 59 times and left her for dead in 1997. After the minister and the soap star left, the 'real life victim', as she was referred to yesterday, told her story.

Her sister Margaret had been married for 25 years to a man who didn't hit her but conducted a mental reign of terror. The husband, Tommy Elden, demanded cups of tea, his dinner cooked a certain way, things to be done immediately.

Then one night in 1997 he decided he did not like his dinner and so he threw his wife out into the back garden. This time Margaret left.

'I had gone to his house with my niece Laura to pick up my sister's stuff. He asked us where Margaret was and then he locked us in,' said Ms Newman. Elden turned and Ms Newman realised he was holding a knife.

He stabbed his daughter and sister-in-law for almost half an hour, retreating only when they played dead. Karen's mobile phone saved her life. She had the foresight to ring 999 while being attacked but couldn't give the address. Her brother-in-law went up to the attic but she knew he had machetes up there – 'he would have had my head off'. She managed to call her husband then and raise the alarm.

Elden was convicted of attempted murder and committed suicide in prison in April.

'I was lucky,' says Ms Newman who had her lungs punctured 12 times and need 14 pints of blood. She knows Elden would have killed her sister if he could have found her. Karen who was 18, has recovered too.

At 37, Ms Newman is training to be a counsellor. The first step is to realise that you could be a victim. 'My sister didn't realise that she was being abused, ' she says. 'So many women don't realise that they are the victims of anything.'

What had I done?

**My husband was a devoted father and successful oil executive.
But he was also a vicious monster who beat me for 20 years . . .**

One in nine British women is severely beaten by her partner every year. The Refuge Crisis Line, the UK's only 24-hour helpline for victims of domestic violence, is now under threat of closure. After an unsuccessful bid for funding to the National Lottery, the charity, which offers specialist advice and secure accommodation in safe houses throughout the country, claims that the lives of thousands of women and children will be put at risk. The psychological and physical scars are often permanent. Here, for the first time, 55-year-old private school teacher Anne Henderson talks about the violence she suffered during her 20-year marriage to an oil executive. By Clare Campbell

Despite all that's happened, I've never thought of myself as a 'battered wife'. The term suggested a cowering woman living in a tower block, covered in cuts and bruises inflicted by a brutish man. I couldn't admit that my professional, charming husband Alex, father of my lovely son and daughter, could be thought of in the same category. Nice middle-class men don't beat up their wives. Or so I believed.

I met Alex at a dinner party. I was only 21 and quickly intrigued by his air of mystery. No one seemed to know much about his background, but I was won over by his good looks and little-boy-lost manner. I wanted to take care of him. We married less than two years later.

I was still very naïve about men, and at first used to blame myself for Alex's mood swings. One moment everything would be fine, and the next, some slight incident would offend him and he'd become cold, distant and hostile.

The first time he was violent towards me was near the end of my first pregnancy, with our daughter Abigail. We had held a dinner party that evening, and after our guests had gone, Alex suddenly noticed that I had left some wine in the bottom of my glass.

At first, he jokingly told me to drink it up. I refused, in the same light-hearted tone, telling him that I'd had enough and was tired and wanted to go to bed. At that, Alex changed completely, forcing my head back by my hair and tipping the dregs of the glass down my throat until I nearly choked.

I was upset, but by the time we went to bed I was left feeling that what had happened was my fault for not obeying him. I tried to put it to the back of my mind, telling myself it would never happen again. Months passed before the next incident. In the meantime, Alex was a loving husband and father and I'd forgotten the violent streak I'd witnessed.

Then, one evening, totally unprovoked, he took a swing at me with his fist, leaving me with a black eye. Alex was with me the next morning when I went to work and heard one of my colleagues ask what had happened.

He stepped forward and laughed, saying: 'She walked into a door.' My friend looked embarrassed, and feeling that this was as good as an admission that he'd hit me, I wondered what Alex was playing at.

After that, the violence continued. But he never again hurt me where it showed. Each attack was frightening, partly because of its unexpectedness and partly because of the confusion it created in my mind. How could someone who was so close to me, someone who had promised to 'love and cherish me' behave so brutally?

I wasted endless hours trying to find some meaning to it all, searching for some explanation for his irrational behaviour. I blamed myself for bringing out the worst in him. I wondered if the attacks were due to alcohol, the result of an over-stressful job, or even the effects of leaving home too young.

I often pleaded with him to tell me what was wrong. But there was never any compromise or discussion. Heavy drinking, which he did frequently, always brought out aggression, usually directed at me. My theory is that he suffered from some deep and inexplicable psychological insecurity about himself or his family background.

Although his family were fairly grand, he'd lie needlessly about them, making out they were even grander. I think he felt he had to boost his self-esteem and he'd do so by boasting about his professional success or, when feeling particularly bad, asserting himself through his violence towards me.

Nothing I did could protect me from it. Sometimes many months would pass between each outburst, so I somehow convinced myself that all was well and it wouldn't happen again.

By this time, we had a son, Alexander. Both our children adored their father. Alex was never violent towards them. If he had been, I'd have left immediately. But they never saw that side of their father's personality.

My husband never hit me in front of them, and I made excuses when they asked me why I was crying, or where my bruises had come from.

In the meantime, Alex's career prospered. His job had always involved a lot of travel, and when Alexander was nine, Alex was offered a job abroad with a high salary which meant the children could go to good boarding schools in Britain.

Both children went away to school and, believing this could be a new start for us, I moved to the Middle East with Alex.

But almost immediately the pattern of violence began again. Now it was accompanied by verbal abuse as well. I would be compared unfavourably with other men's wives, criticised for everything from my appearance and driving skills to my choice of friends and failure to satisfy his sexual needs.

Any assertive behaviour on my part would make things worse, provoking him into an even deeper fury.

As the attacks grew more frequent (they always did when the children were away) I resorted to coping strategies – a sleeping bag kept in the boot of my car; my handbag, keys and money left close to the front door, ready for escape should I feel the situation becoming dangerous.

Often I spent the night in the car rather than risk returning home. Once I slept in the children's toy cupboard. It seemed better than asking friends for help and having to admit the truth. But I always went back. In the light of day, things seemed less frightening.

Alex never appeared to remember what had happened. There was never an apology, no references to the event. Sometimes, if it hadn't been for the bruises and the physical pain, I could almost have believed I had imagined the episode.

Looking back, I wonder how I could ever have stayed. Foremost was my concern for my children. I didn't think I could provide for them financially on my own and, although Alex did not regard the family as a 'priority', I felt that it would be unfair to destroy his relationship with his children with the sordid details of a court case.

I was also frightened of not being believed. To the outside world, Alex was a successful man in a respectable profession. He had a great deal of charm and plausibility. When things were going his way, he could also be loving and affectionate towards me. I suppose that was what kept me

hooked – the belief that he would remain like that all the time.

But then his mood could swing without warning. Out would pour a torrent of insults, irrational accusations and threats and I'd retreat into a world of confusion once more.

What had I done? In reality, I'd done nothing, but he had a knack of making me feel guilty. He'd never back down and admit he was wrong.

Occasionally I'd take a stand, determined to have some say in matters that affected my future. But then I risked incurring his anger, which could, and often did, lead to a frenzied attack.

Whenever I confronted him with the bruises as evidence, he denied having caused them, or claimed that he 'couldn't remember' what had happened. When I suggested he needed help, he got angrier.

Eventually, it seemed easier to bury my head in the sand. I convinced myself that he'd never seriously hurt me, but the attacks took their toll on my health. I became nervous and depressed, I had nightmares, spells of insomnia and I found it increasingly difficult to talk to people on the phone.

It was an emotional paralysis – I felt no blazing anger and no longer shed any tears. All that was left was an overwhelming sense of hopelessness.

Alex and I moved again, this time to the Caribbean, again because of a better job offer. By this time I felt I was living a double life.

Whenever I was at work teaching, with my children, or with friends, I acted like the perfect wife, hosting cocktail parties, smiling and talking to strangers as though there was nothing wrong in my life. This continued for the next four years. Then one night, Alex finally went too far. Abigail and Alexander had caught a flight to return to their boarding schools that afternoon.

Alex had heard a few weeks earlier that we would be returning to Britain, and we arranged to have a farewell drink with friends. I was feeling that life might be possible again. Alex had not been violent towards me for some time.

I went to sleep that evening peaceful and optimistic for the future. Suddenly I was woken by an intense awareness of imminent peril. Alex was standing over me with such a murderous look in his eyes that I knew my life was in danger.

Grabbing the nearest object to hand, I lashed out to protect myself with the bedside light. That was a huge mistake, because it made Alex even angrier. He launched himself at me in an appalling physical assault. As he was much heavier built than me, I knew I didn't stand a chance.

I cannot remember screaming, but I must have done. For suddenly, our neighbours were pounding on the door. There had been several assaults on women by strangers during the previous weeks, and we had all been warned to be on the look-out.

Obviously, my neighbours believed me to have been the victim of one of these attackers – not my own husband.

Alex stopped hitting me just long enough for me to rush to the door. It was clear from my friends' faces that they could see what had happened. I think even Alex was shocked at what he had done.

That night, I stayed at a neighbour's house. The following morning I went to the doctor and was later flown to hospital on the mainland. There, for the first time, I told a doctor of my 19 years of marital violence. He was shocked and gave me a medical report on my injuries – to use as evidence.

I was told by friends that Alex had returned to Britain full of remorse. This assault seemed to bring him to his senses and make him admit his bad behaviour.

He wrote to me and to a friend of mine, saying how terribly he'd treated me, and how much he regretted it.

Even at this point, I was ready to forgive if I could trust him to change. I was adamant that he needed help rather than punishment. After a few months' separation, I returned to him. The children, who were away at school, never knew I'd been in hospital.

Alex voluntarily sought help and was referred to a psychiatrist. He also gave up alcohol and seemed set to put the past behind us and embark at last on a normal life.

But although he never again laid a finger on me, his selfishness hadn't changed. His recovery took priority over family commitments and I was again left to juggle responsibility for the children, home and a full-time job.

I felt his concern was more for the possible damage to his reputation than the damage to me and the family. Once back on the career path and sure I was not going to bring charges, Alex's old attitudes reappeared.

By this time I had to admit that any trust and respect I had once held for him had been destroyed. When a new job came up that meant him moving, I chose, in the face of threats of what he'd do if I spoke about past events, to let him go alone.

Although I no longer live in fear of attack, I feel cheated of the friendship and emotional security marriage promised

---

We divorced seven years ago. Alex married again within nine months. I felt particularly bitter when our children attended his wedding, but having always protected them from his true nature, I couldn't blame them.

In many ways, I've been lucky. I suffered only minor long-term damage from the physical abuse, although the scars of the verbal battering have taken longer to heal. For a long time, I alternated between pain and anger, feeling at last all those emotions I had suppressed for so long.

But although I no longer live in fear of attack, I feel cheated of the friendship and emotional security marriage promised.

Alex was offered all the help and support he needed to change his ways. Instead, he acted like a true coward by running away and refusing to take responsibility for what he had done.

He was arrogant enough to believe he wasn't accountable to anyone. Too many violent men get away without facing the consequences of their actions. But it is often the women who live with them who are to blame for this.

Whatever our reasons for staying silent, it is only when we are prepared to speak out that we cease to be victims. But this will not happen until women feel society can offer them some protection against their partners. The real problem is not one of battered women, but of violent men.

• Refuge 24-hour Crisis Line: 0990 995 443; Refuge Donation Line: 0171-395 7709

© The Daily Mail
April, 1998

How many seek refuge?

The Women's Aid Annual Survey

As part of our information programme Women's Aid regularly explores the number and profile of women and children accessing Women's Aid and other refuge and support services across England. Some of our key findings are listed below.

This year our annual survey of refuge services in England (based on those using the service in 1996/7) indicated that:

- There were 54,500 admissions to refuges during the year. Of this figure approximately 32,017 were children and 22,492 were women.
- Over the year calls to refuges and support services from women experiencing domestic violence totalled 145,317 (this figure is estimated – some refuges give estimated and not exact figures).
- 67,192 of these calls were from women seeking refuge and 69,875 calls were from women requesting advice and support only.
- The largest group (41%) of women using refuge services were aged between 26 and 35 years. Nearly 25% were 19-25 years and nearly 20% were 36-45 years of age.
- On leaving refuge accommodation 29% were successfully rehoused in either local authority or housing association properties and only 6% went into the private rented sector. Nearly 10% went to stay with friends and relatives and 15% moved on to another refuge. Just over 12% returned home with an injunction against their violent partner, but at least 20% actually returned to their abuser.

© Women's Aid Federation of England (WAFE)

Crackdown on domestic violence

TV advertisement uses Oxo model to encourage middle-class children to report abuse in the home as part of government initiative

By Nicholas Watt, Political Correspondent

Middle-class children are to be encouraged to report violence against their mothers and sisters at home as part of an initiative by the Government to tackle domestic abuse across all social classes.

A television advertisement will target middle-class children by portraying a domestic scene similar to the successful Oxo advertisements, which turns sour when the father verbally abuses his wife.

In the advertisement, to be screened before the 9.30pm watershed over Christmas, a wife waits at home with her two children for her husband to return from work. When he appears he asks where his dinner is and she tells him it will be a few minutes late because she has been busy. He becomes verbally aggressive, berating his wife for failing to perform her role. The advertisement will be screened in Scotland as a pilot for the rest of Britain, and will contain a helpline for children to phone if a woman in their house has been abused.

Helen Liddell, the Scottish Office minister with responsibility for women's issues, said yesterday that the £600,000 advertisement had been designed to look like the Oxo series because domestic violence occurred across all social classes. Ms Liddell, speaking at the launch of Delivering for Women, the government initiative to improve the lives of women, said the Women's Unit had made the fight against domestic abuse one of its priorities.

Recent research found that one in four women experience violence at home at some point. The 1996 British Crime Survey found 44 per cent of all violent crimes experienced by women in 1995 were domestic.

Ms Liddell said: 'Domestic abuse knows no boundaries of social class or social group. We have to dispel the myth that it only occurs in criminal classes or at specific social levels. A survey has shown an appallingly high proportion of young people of both sexes think violence is sometimes excusable. Domestic abuse is never excusable, we must provide a long-term solution to tackle this attitude.'

On the wider issue of improving women's lives, Baroness Jay of Paddington, the Minister for Women, said that the Government was determined to sweep away barriers which prevent women from reaching their potential. She cited a series of initiatives launched by the Government in the past year, including improved child care provision and providing more family-friendly employment policies.

At yesterday's launch, Lady Jay announced that the Women's Unit had decided to target teenage girls because research shows they fall behind boys after out-performing

them throughout their early years at school. There has been a substantial improvement in girls' performance at GCSEs and A levels, but 'then something seems to happen, and they do not fulfil their earlier potential', said Tessa Jowell, the women's minister in the Commons.

Improving women's lives

- Investigation into why teenage girls fall behind boys after out-performing them in their early school years. The former Spice Girl Geri Halliwell and the actress Emma Thompson may be signed up as role models for teenagers.

- Analysis into discrepancy between men's and women's income to be published next year. Women in full-time employment are still paid 80 per cent of men's earnings despite increase in number of women working.

- Extension of child care provision. In the past year the Government has launched the national child care strategy with the aim of providing high-quality child care for all children up to the age of 14.

- Improvement in family-friendly employment policies. Government will work in partnership with employers' organisations to help men and women fit family commitments around their work.

- Tackling domestic abuse across all classes. Television advertisement will raise awareness of abuse among children.

- Improvement in women's representation. Government is committed to a 50:50 ratio of men and women in public appointments.

Domestic violence

Domestic violence does not only affect women, but can have severely damaging consequences for children

Key points

- Many families live with violence, but this receives less attention than other forms of violence and may be seen by some as a 'normal' part of family life.
- The impact of domestic violence on children needs to be far better recognised.
- One in five child abuse cases dealt with by the NSPCC involves domestic violence.
- In nine out of 10 cases, children are present in the home while violence is going on.
- In about half of cases there is violence to children too.
- Violence within families may go on for years and affect children physically, psychologically, emotionally and socially.
- More than a quarter of Barnardo's projects are working with families affected by domestic violence.

Background

The largest recent increase in recorded violent crime has been in domestic violence, with 3.4 times more incidents of domestic violence reported in 1995 than in 1981. Domestic violence largely concerns violence by men to their female partner or ex-partner. It includes physical, sexual and emotional attacks.

Many people think that domestic violence is an issue that only affects women, yet in 90 per cent of cases, children are in the same or next room while violence is going on.[1] They may be hurt trying to stop the violence, or may be the target of abuse themselves. Between 40 and 60 per cent of all domestic violence cases involve violence to children as well as the mother.[2]

In extreme cases domestic violence can lead to the death of the child or a parent. More than 40 per cent of women killed in England and Wales in 1995 were killed by a current or former partner or lover.[3] Many public inquiries into the deaths of children in recent years have shown that the men responsible for the child's death have a history of violence towards their female partners.[4]

Violence in the home may go on for years and affects children in a number of ways. Even if they are not physically harmed, children may suffer lasting emotional and psychological damage as a result of witnessing violence. They may be encouraged to take part in bullying or threatening the mother, or be threatened by the father as a way of controlling the mother.

Very young children may show physical signs of distress such as bedwetting, stomach aches and sleep disturbances. Older children can become very withdrawn or exhibit extreme behaviour as a result of witnessing abuse, and they may feel they are to blame for what is happening. They may become over-protective of their mother, refusing to leave her and affecting their education and social development. Teenage children may become involved in drugs or alcohol; some young people run away from home and others may make suicide attempts.[5]

Women and children fleeing the home as a result of domestic violence are at high risk of homelessness, many having to live in temporary accommodation or refuges. More than 30,000 children were recorded as living in refuges in 1994/5.[6] For many families, issues of race, culture and religion can add to the difficulty of escaping domestic violence.

If they have to move to escape violence, children will have to cope with a new home in a new area, a new school and leaving family and friends behind. They may spend long periods in temporary accommodation, with damaging consequences for their development (see Barnardo's Briefing: *Homeless Families*). Despite the violence, they may still love and miss their dad.

What Barnardo's is doing

A 1996 audit of Barnardo's projects found that 42 per cent reported domestic violence as an issue, with one-fifth saying it was a frequent part of their work. More than a quarter were offering support for affected children.

Barnardo's aims to alleviate the long-term effects of domestic violence on children through counselling and family support services. Many mothers continue to provide love and stability for their children in very difficult circumstances, and

Barnardo's aims to strengthen their ability to cope. Where the mother's ability to look after her children has been undermined by the stress of living with fear, we try to help her improve her confidence and self-esteem so that she can protect herself and their children from violence.

Some projects offer group programmes to help women make plans to tackle what is happening to them, giving them the chance to meet others in the same situation and encouraging them to take control of their lives.

Projects also offer practical help, such as advice and information on housing, financial and legal issues. There is counselling for children to help them talk through their feelings and experiences, together with play sessions, after school clubs, holidays and outings.

Barnardo's does a small amount of work with men who have been violent towards their partners, with the aim of helping them to change their behaviour, and develop their approach to personal relationships and being a father.

Together with the NSPCC and the Bristol University Domestic Violence Unit, Barnardo's has produced a training pack, *Making an Impact – Children and Domestic Violence*, which is aimed at raising awareness of the impact of domestic violence and equipping people who work with children with the skills and knowledge to support children through a deeply traumatic time.

References
1   *Domestic violence and social care,* Social Services Inspectorate, 1995
2. Witnessing spouse abuse and experiencing physical abuse, HM Hughes, D Parkinson and M Vargo, *Journal of Family Violence,* 1989
3. *British Crime Survey,* 1996
4. *Child deaths in contexts of domestic violence,* M O'Hara, 1994
5   *The Hidden Victims – Children and Domestic Violence,* C Abrahams, 1994; *To Grow Up in the Vicinity of Violence,* K Weinehall, 1997; *Behind Closed Doors,* M Straus, RJ Gelles and SK Steinmetz, 1980
6. *Survey of refugee groups 1994/95,* Women's Aid Federation, 1995

The cruel truth about the way the courts treat kids

As a 10-year-old victim said, 'Anyone can father a child, but that doesn't mean they can be a dad'

By Yasmin Alibhai-Brown

You are a mother of small children. A neighbour comes to the door and asks whether he can take your children out to the park with his own. You know that he is a brute who beats up his wife and that his kids always look frightened. The wife has ended up in hospital with face injuries. You would, I expect, shut the door in his face fast enough (with luck) to catch his nose.

But if this man were the father of your kids and you were the woman who had ended up with broken bones, slashes and burns, you would not have the right to shut that door – not unless a judge had granted you an injunction to keep him away from your children. Most of the time this does not happen, according to an agonising *Dispatches* television programme broadcast recently on Channel 4.

Viewers will be shocked to learn that our judicial system does not take domestic violence into account when deciding whether or not a child should carry on seeing a non-custodial parent after separation. With 160,000 divorces a year, thousands of children are affected by this failure of the law. The partner can be protected from further abuse, but vulnerable children, at least until they grow up to be teenagers, are forced to see these men even if it causes them untold terror.

Our judicial system does not take domestic violence into account when deciding whether or not a child should carry on seeing a non-custodial parent

Eight-year-old Timothy (not his real name) cannot understand why. He never wants to see his 'first daddy', because he is horrible and because he remembers him hitting his mother. Yet Timothy's father, who had been kept for years in a psychiatric hospital, won the right to see him. It took several further court cases for Timothy to get the protection he needed.

Two young sisters, also featured in the documentary, describe how their father bangs their heads down on the desk or stabs them with forks if they make a mistake with their multiplication tables, and how they dream of him dying.

Yet the court ruled that the girls 'benefited' from seeing their father. Some mothers have been imprisoned for refusing to follow such rulings. Sarah, a fragile woman with her pain bone-dry, recalls how she pleaded with court officials but failed to stop her husband getting access to Jack (three) and Nina (four), who frolic on a home video as she tells this story. The children were eventually killed by her husband, who then committed suicide. 'It is too late,' she says, her voice so gentle that you hardly hear her.

All this, you understand, is done in the 'best interests of the child'. Our society believes that a child will thrive only if both parents are present in his or her life. In an ideal world, and if the parents are conscientious, it is not a bad principle.

But it is insane and dangerous to make this into a pivotal, quasi-religious belief. In any case, it hardly stands up to any kind of rational scrutiny. If two biological parents are so essential, are children brought up by widows eternally damned? Would we allow a cruel adoptive father to have a child, because any father is better than none?

Taking this line negates morality and personal responsibility for actions. What are we teaching future generations about abusive behaviour within families if we tell children in such families that their love and loyalty for their brutalised mothers and their own suffering in the hands of a violent father are of no consequence? That, in effect, a single sperm cell gives a man immunity from social condemnation and inviolable rights over his product? We know from studies conducted in the United States since the Forties that juvenile offenders often have violent and alcoholic fathers. Angela Phillips, in her book, *The Trouble With Boys*, also points out that a man who beats up his partner 'is going to teach his son that this is normal behaviour'.

Most of all, we need to talk to the children and to treat them as equal citizens in our society

---

What is even more extra-ordinary is that we now have in place the Children Act, which was supposed to give vulnerable children a half-decent chance to make a go of their lives. It turns out that, in this area, the Act is more or less ineffective.

The first-ever research about children in contact with violent fathers after separation shows that many of these children are neglected and beaten and some are sexually abused during visits. In a quarter of the cases, the fathers were drunk and one in seven of the children was left on its own.

What makes it worse – and the children say this – is that the mothers are not there to safeguard them. Dr Lorraine Radford, an expert on children and domestic violence, is convinced that we need a radical rethink of the law in order to stop the legally sanctioned victimisation of already traumatised children.

Why have we allowed this situation to develop? I think the reasons lie deep within our social attitudes to children. We still think of them as our possessions, com-modities and chattels, to be divided up neatly after divorce. The Dickensian father may have become the stuff of costume drama, but the Victorian assumptions of paternal power still determine our laws and behaviour. In our wisdom we rely on the truism: 'He is, after all, the father.'

This means that whatever he does, however bad he is, some distant moment of ejaculation gives a father rights that should never, ever, be taken away. As one articulate 10-year-old points out in the programme: 'Anyone can father a child. But that doesn't mean they can be a dad.'

We need urgently to change the law, although the Lord Chancellor's Department appears to have no plans for this in the near future. According to some senior family lawyers, it may even be possible to use the existing Children Act to change practice by introducing new guidelines for judges and court welfare officers who make the assessments on whether or not children should see their fathers. These officers are not trained in child psychology nor the effects of do-mestic violence. Jack and Nina died because the officer in charge did not understand the psychotic condition of their father.

But, most of all, we need to talk to the children and to treat them as equal citizens in our society. They are individuals who must be entitled to participate in decisions about parental contact. This will not happen unless we understand that we have no absolute rights over our children, but that as caring adults we must promote and protect their rights. We may give them life, but their lives are not our property. And in the end, you have to earn the privilege of parenting by proving that you are worth it. © *The Independent April, 1999*

Domestic violence: a rural and urban crime

Are we in danger of giving victims in rural areas the message that domestic violence does not exist? Janet Stephens, Co-ordinator of Victim Support Cotswold, argues that we need to understand the differences between rural and urban areas, where crimes are the same but the situation is not.

There is an urban belief that car ownership indicates wealth. But for rural families who live in villages with no daily bus service, and who can't afford taxis, a car is a necessity to get to work, school, the health centre or the shops. Some families can only afford to run a vehicle by making great sacrifices. Others have to struggle without what amounts to a lifeline, not least if they are victims of domestic violence.

Can you imagine the isolation felt by such a woman, particularly if she has young children and is beaten regularly by her husband, who may also be out of work or an alcoholic?

She has no money, no transport and possibly no phone. She feels there is no protection, nor anyone to help her. She cannot even run into the road to flag down a passing car because it could be ages before anyone drives by.

It's a far cry from the traditional chocolate-box image of the Cotswolds which attracts visitors from all over the world. But the Cotswolds is an area of extremes. The large number of wealthy households helps to raise the average income as well as house prices, at the same time as it hides the abject poverty and lack of affordable housing that exist alongside.

It costs 50 per cent more to buy a two-bedroomed house in the Cotswolds than it does in Gloucester town and many families find it difficult enough to find their first home. Re-housing for victims of domestic violence can seem almost impossible. Even if the Council has social housing available, it might be miles from friends and family.

So the victim who manages to escape domestic violence can then be faced with increased isolation. She may also face increased poverty, as she tries to live on a single income or reduced benefits. Wages in rural areas are low and there is evidence of a greater sense of the stigma of claiming benefits and / or a lack of awareness of some of the benefits which may be available.

Rural poverty is not just financial, there may also be poverty of service provision. As well as lack of a bus service, many rural villages have few or none of the services urban dwellers take for granted, such as community facilities for education, local health care and neighbourhood shops, as well as the drop-in facilities and refuges that provide temporary or permanent shelter for urban victims of domestic violence.

This isolation and poverty is real and one that is experienced by those who live in thousands of rural backwaters across the country. It is emphasised further when individuals become victims of domestic violence. Yet when few support services are provided, we are in danger of giving victims in rural areas the message that domestic violence does not exist.

This is where Victim Support plays such a large part in helping a rural victim, for example, with transport to visit a solicitor. Simple things can be of paramount importance, as it can represent the start of a long climb back to self-respect and being able to cope.

But it is not unusual for a volunteer to make round-trips of 60-80 miles, which is why we must recognise that, although the crime is the same, whether in town or country, the practical help and support are quite different and possibly more demanding for rural volunteers.

When urban dwellers enjoy a day in the country, a sunny day in spring or summer, with birds singing, bluebells in the woods and a jolly pub to lunch in, they should remember there is another side of the coin: grey skies, driving rain, mud up to your backside and dark from 3.30pm, with no street lighting and nowhere to go from the violence that for some women is always there.

Case study

Twenty-six-year-old Sue* had been married to Brian* for two years and they had a 10-month-old daughter Kerri.* Before her marriage and for a short time afterwards Sue had been a friendly, outgoing person who enjoyed going out with Brian and her friends. Soon after their marriage Brian started to get sulky and moody if Sue talked to anyone else, male or female, and if she wanted to meet any of her friends. Soon he became more and more possessive and jealous and the sulks turned to verbal abuse and physical assaults. Sue changed her behaviour to try to keep him happy and she became quiet and withdrawn, not able to tell anyone about her situation. It became harder and harder to placate Brian, and then on one occasion when they were with a group of friends 'he had a go at me and put me down in front of them. I felt humiliated, upset and angry because I hadn't done anything to deserve it.' She decided that she had had enough and took Kerri and moved back to live with her parents.

A few evenings later, whilst Sue's parents were away, Brian went round and threatened Sue with a knife. 'I was terrified, I thought he was going to kill me. I kept trying to get away from him but he kept pulling me down by my hair and flinging me against the wall. I could hear Kerri screaming upstairs but I couldn't get away. It seemed to go on forever while he called me names and kept saying he'd do me in.' Eventually he threw her to the ground and then left. Sue, shaking and sobbing, rushed upstairs to calm Kerri down, and then phoned the police.

After she had given her statement she lay awake at night fearful that Brian would return, because although he had been arrested that night no one had told Sue. Sue was too frightened to stay on her own so she spent the next few days staying with friends and relatives. It was at this point that a Victim Support volunteer contacted her by phone. Up until then no one had given her any information about the police investigation, and the volunteer was able to help with this.

The volunteer visited several times, during these visits Sue was gradually able to talk about the relationship, her fears and the future. The volunteer was also able to help her with practical problems such as help with housing through liaising with the Housing Department.

Sue had given a statement to the police and Brian was charged with Actual Bodily Harm, so Sue had to appear in the Magistrate's Court to give evidence against him. 'I was so scared because I would have

to see him again and I didn't want to. But I was determined to go through with it because if I didn't he would get away with it and might do it again to someone else or me. I was glad that the Victim Support volunteer was going to court with me.'

Sue will never forget the day of the court case: Brian watched her arrive, there was a long delay before the start of the case, and because Brian glared at her whilst he was giving evidence Sue got confused and upset. 'I was so glad the volunteer was able to help me through it, she took me into a separate waiting room and accompanied me into the court to give me moral support.'

It was late afternoon when the magistrates announced a guilty verdict. Sue was relieved and happy:

'it's like having a huge weight lifted off my shoulders. I was glad that people believed me. I am now looking forward to the future with Kerri in our new home.'

*   * names have been changed
• The original report by Janet Stephens of Victim Support Cotswold appeared in the *Victim Support Magazine*, the magazine of the national charity Victim Support, and is reproduced here with thanks. Victim Support operates a telephone Supportline for anyone who has suffered the effects of crime, regardless of whether the crime has been reported. Telephone 0845 3030900, open 9am-9pm Mon-Fri and 9am-7pm Sat/Sun.

© Victim Support
Autumn, 1998

Violence against women

Information from the World Health Organisation (WHO)

While violence against women has become widely recognised as a major issue of women's human rights, more recently there has also been growing awareness of the impact of violence on women's mental and physical health. Violence against women in families dramatically increases their risk of poor health, with studies consistently reporting negative and far-reaching effects. According to the World Bank, rape and domestic violence account for an estimated 5-16% (depending upon region) of the

healthy years of life which are lost to women of reproductive age.

Numerous studies have shown that the most pervasive form of gender violence is violence against women by their intimate male partners or ex-partners, including the physical, mental and sexual abuse of women and sexual abuse of children and adolescents. Countering these forms of domestic violence, together with violence against women in conflict situations, is the main focus of WHO's activities in this area.

Definition

There is no universally accepted definition of violence against women.

However, a group of international experts convened by WHO in February 1996 agreed that the definition adopted by the United Nations General Assembly provides a useful framework for the Organisation's activities.

The Declaration on the Elimination of Violence against Women (1993) defines violence against women as 'any act of gender-based violence that results in, or is likely to result in, physical, sexual or mental harm or suffering to women, including threats of such acts, coercion or arbitrary deprivation of liberty, whether occurring in public or in private life.'

This encompasses, *inter alia*, 'physical, sexual and psychological violence occurring in the family and in the general community, including battering, sexual abuse of children, dowry-related violence, rape, female genital mutilation and other traditional practices harmful to women, non-spousal violence and violence related to exploitation, sexual harassment and intimidation at work, in educational institutions and elsewhere, trafficking in women, forced prostitution, and violence perpetrated or condoned by the state'.

Prevalence

Reliable data on the prevalence of violence against women by their partners are scarce, especially in developing countries, but a growing body of research confirms its pervasiveness. Approximately 40 valid population-based quantitative studies, conducted in 24 countries on four continents, revealed a range of 20% to 50% of women being victims of physical abuse by their partners at some time in their lives. On average, these same studies found that 50-60% of women who are abused by their partners are raped by them as well. These and other studies on the problem also show that:

- the perpetrators of violence against women are almost exclusively men;
- women are at greatest risk of violence from men whom they know;
- women and girls are the most frequent victims of violence within the family and between intimate partners;
- physical abuse in intimate relationships is almost always accompanied by severe psychological and verbal abuse;
- the response of many professionals and social institutions has been to either blame or ignore the victims.

Violence against women in families may also be one of the most important precipitating factors of female suicide, and is closely associated with homicide. Global evidence suggests that most homicides of women are committed by a male partner or ex-partner.

Violence against women in situations of conflict and against women refugees also constitutes a major problem. It is estimated that 75% of the 18 million refugees in the world today are women and girls; most are malnourished and exposed to disease and many are the victims of violence or rape, which often do permanent damage to their health.

Mental health consequences

Among the numerous adverse health consequences of violence against women, psychological wounds may well be the most severe, and require more time to heal than wounds to the body. As one victim observed to the Bombay Women's Centre in India:

'The body mends soon enough. Only the scars remain... But the wounds inflicted upon the soul take much longer to heal. And each time I relive these moments, they start bleeding all over again. The broken spirit has taken the longest to mend; the damage to the personality may be the most difficult to overcome.'

Depression, anxiety, psychosomatic symptoms, compulsive and obsessive disorders, low self-esteem, eating problems, sexual dysfunction and post-traumatic stress disorder (PTSD) are all common to victims of partner violence. Victims of violence are likely to develop behaviours that are self-injurious, such as substance abuse and smoking.

Violence has also been associated with greater sexual risk-taking among adolescents, and the development of sexual problems in adulthood.

In the United States, a research survey found that women with a history of sexual assault were nearly twice as likely to have sought mental health care during the six months preceding the survey than men and women who had not been sexually assaulted. Other US studies have shown that a history of rape or assault is a stronger predictor of physician visits and medical costs than any other variable.

WHO activities

The consultation on violence against women which WHO organised in February 1996 recommended that WHO recognise psychological/mental abuse as being integral to violence against women in families, and that the Organisation develop and test a methodology for measuring it. The body identified information gaps and made recommendations for action in research, including the development of appropriate research methodologies and interventions to prevent, and address the consequences of violence. These are currently being implemented as part of a new WHO initiative. Specific activities include a multi-country research project on the prevalence and health consequences of violence against women; development of a global database to improve accessibility to information; and ongoing advocacy with health profession organisations to incorporate the issue of violence against women into their public health activities.

The WHO Global Commission on Women's Health, a high-level advocacy body which promotes women's health issues nationally and internationally, focussed on the issue of violence against women at its most recent meeting in April 1996. Among the positions it adopted was that WHO should advocate for zero tolerance of violence against women, with particular emphasis on domestic violence and violence against women in conflict situations. A working group appointed by the Commission will study mechanisms for monitoring implementation of existing human rights treaties with respect to violence against women, and promote compliance with them.

For further information, please contact Health Communications and Public Relations, World Health Organisation, Geneva. Telephone (00 41 22) 791 3221 or Fax (00 41 22) 791 4858.

- All World Health Organisation press releases, fact sheets and features can be obtained on Internet on the WHO home page http://www.who.ch/

© WHO/OMS, 1998
August, 1996

Domestic violence – who can help?

Are you being abused by your partner? Do you need a safe place to stay, away from your abuser? If you need to leave home due to physical, emotional or sexual abuse, or just want to talk to someone about your experiences, Women's Aid can help you.

What is domestic violence?

Domestic violence is the physical, emotional, sexual or mental abuse of one person (usually a woman) by another, with whom they have or have had an intimate relationship. Domestic violence is rarely a one-off event. It tends to escalate in frequency and severity over time.

It can be physical and can include: slapping, punching, beating, kicking, knife wounds – often leading to permanent injuries and sometimes death.

It can be sexual – this could include being forced to have sex against your will, sexual degradation, forcing sex in ways that hurt and abuse you.

It can also be emotional and mental, including: constant criticism, telling you that you are useless, ugly, worthless, or humiliating you. Threatening to kill or harm you or the children, intimidation, bullying, being locked in or kept in isolation away from family and friends, not allowing you any money, food, sleep, and freedom. Being made a prisoner in your own home.

Everyone has the right to be safe in their own home, yet tens of thousands of women and children in this country are regularly subjected to intimidation and violence.

What is the Women's Aid National Helpline?

The Women's Aid National Helpline offers support, help and informa-

tion to women who are experiencing, or who have experienced, domestic violence. You can call the Helpline and talk to a volunteer in confidence. You may want to call because you need help finding somewhere to stay, or you may need some advice about legal matters. But many women who call the Helpline just want someone to talk to and share their experiences with. Your call will be confidential, you can talk for as long as you need and as often as you like. There will always be someone to help you.

What is a refuge?

A refuge is a safe house which offers temporary accommodation for women and their children. There are about 250 refuges in the UK which provide a place of safety for any woman who needs to escape violence, married or single, with or without children. Many of these refuges are run by Women's Aid groups. Women's Aid refuges are run by women for women and children. Some are run by a combination of paid staff and volunteers or volunteers only. Women's Aid refuges do not have 'live in' wardens

who are in charge and women staying in the refuge can have a say in how the refuge should be run. Many women come to refuges for a break from the violence. Refuges provide a breathing space where decisions can be made free from pressure and fear. Women can stay as long as they want, this can be anything from a few days to several months. The refuge will help you if you need to find a more permanent place to stay.

Will we be safe?

Refuge addresses and telephone numbers are secret, so that it is difficult for the abuser to find a woman who has left home. You don't have to choose a refuge in your own area, if you want to we can arrange a safe place miles away from your abuser.

Who can stay at a refuge?

Any woman who is experiencing domestic violence can go to a refuge, but you don't have to prove that you've been abused. It doesn't matter if you are married or single, and you don't have to have any children. If you do have children, Women's Aid

There is a hiding place

The Silent Witness Appeal has been launched by Refuge, to help children suffering because of domestic violence. Sandra Horley of Refuge explains – and reveals their exclusive survey findings

Tom is one of thousands of children suffering from Post-Traumatic Stress Disorder, a result of observing extreme violence. His terrifying story is told below, in his own words. For most, this is not brutality they have seen abroad or even on the streets where they live, but is experienced in their own homes. Tom is a silent witness of domestic abuse and he is not alone. Each year, Refuge receives 20,000 calls from women. A study of the appeals for help received by our 24-Hour National Crisis Line in October gives a startling insight into what goes on behind closed doors:

- 85 per cent of the callers have children.
- 38 per cent are in immediate danger; terrified for their lives and their children.
- 75 per cent of the youngsters have witnessed hitting, shaking, stabbing, verbal abuse and rape or sexual assault.
- 62 per cent of the children witnessing such treatment have experiences ranging from sexual abuse, assault, verbal and mental abuse.
- 50 per cent of callers have contacted the police for help, but 83 per cent found them unhelpful.

Our trained staff and volunteers give specialist advice and support 24 hours a day, every day of the year. We offer people secure accommodation through a network of safe houses across the country.

Our ground-breaking child psychology programme utilises professionals within the refuges who help unlock the pain, terror and guilt felt by children.

Domestic violence is a national epidemic affecting the lives of hundreds of thousands of women every day. One female in four will have been physically assaulted by her partner at some point.

Yet society still refuses to treat domestic violence seriously. Many people believe it's most likely to occur in working-class homes, especially if the man has been drinking. But that's just not true. Abusers come from all social backgrounds. I've counselled women who've been abused by doctors, bank managers, lawyers and business executives. Many men hit their partners when they're stone cold sober.

So what can we do?

The first step is to ensure that police arrest and charge men guilty of domestic violence. We must educate people and emphasise that it is a crime. We want to provide specialist services. To do that we need more funding, to help us to help them.

Happily, as time passes, most of the children who make it to Refuge are able to put the violence, fear and intimidation behind them. We see their tears turn into smiles.

How Refuge helped one child to smile again

My name is Tom and I am 12. I used to live in a refuge, but now we (Mum and my sister Katie, 10) have our own house, but because of Dad we have to keep our address a secret.

I first remember Dad hitting Mum when I was about eight. Me and Katie were playing in our bedroom, we heard Dad shouting and swearing at Mum, he did it all the time. We went to the top of the stairs, and Mum was crying and screaming 'no'. We could hear Dad hitting her and calling her a bitch. Katie looked scared so we went back to our room.

One day when we were watching telly, Dad came in and started swearing at Mum and told us to go to bed. Mum told him not to take it out on us. Then Dad got really angry and started slapping her. Katie started to cry and Dad shouted at her. Mum told him to stop and then he punched Mum in the face again and again and pulled her hair.

Mum was crying and so was Katie. I didn't know what to do. Dad didn't stop hitting Mum. She was on the floor. Dad shouted at Katie, telling her to stop crying, but she didn't and he banged our heads together. I try not to remember it, it makes me feel bad.

I got bad school reports because I couldn't do the work. I found it hard to concentrate because I worried that when I went home, Dad would shout at us and start hurting Mum.

Last year, we went to a refuge, which is a secret house for mums and children.

At first, I thought Dad hit Mum because me and Katie used to leave our games in the lounge. I thought it was our fault. Then I found out that other dads hit mums and it wasn't our fault. At the refuge, Janice [a child psychologist] used to talk to us about what happened. At first, I didn't talk very much but I could do other things like play with the toys and we would draw pictures of what we were feeling, we would draw the scary things that happened at home.

Katie used to play with the toy house and the policeman, she made the policeman take Dad away. We learned that dads shouldn't hit mums and us, it's wrong. I know now that if someone is hurting Mum again, we should go to a safe place and telephone for help.

After a few weeks, we started to join in with other children and we learned how to tell about our secrets. I don't feel as weird as I used to and it's much easier to talk about those things.

It's still hard at school sometimes, because I have bad days [Tom has epilepsy] and have to take my tablets. Katie finds it hard to do her homework sometimes and I try and help her.

Now we live in a new house. I'm happy because Dad isn't around and

Mum smiles a lot now, and I can talk to her about anything. She works and Katie and me still go to the groups [Refuge's children's groups]. I feel safe because we have special telephone numbers to call if there is a problem [like being discovered] and we still see Janice.

Katie doesn't draw sad faces any more, but smiley ones. I can smile on the inside now.

Children's names have been changed to protect their identity.

• Refuge's Donation Line for the Silent Witness Appeal is 0171-385 7709. Send donations to: Refuge, 2 Maltravers Street, London WC2R 3EE. The Refuge 24-hour National Crisis Line is on: 0990 995 443. © *The Express December, 1998*

What can I expect from the police?

This article explains what you should be able to expect from the police if you need protection from violence in your home

'It is the immediate duty of police officers who are called to a domestic violence incident to secure the protection of the victim and any children from further abuse and then to consider what action should be taken against the offender.'
Home Office Circular C60/1990.

What should I do in an emergency?

You have the right to protection from violence just like anyone else in any other situation, and you should call the police (dial 999).

What should the police do?

• Respond as quickly as possible and enforce the law.
• Ensure that you are safe.
• Speak to you and your partner separately so that you don't feel intimidated.
• Refuse to accept your partner's excuses for his violent behaviour or his explanations of why you 'deserved' it.
• Arrest the man where there is

evidence of an assault or other offence.
• Know if there is an order in force and arrest the man if he has broken the terms of an order which carried the power of arrest or his bail conditions.
• Arrange for medical treatment for you if you need it.
• Give you information about local sources of help, e.g. Women's Aid.
• If they are not able to arrest and remove your partner and you feel too afraid to stay in the house,

In some police forces, there are officers with special responsibility for 'domestic violence'. Some have special units called 'Domestic Violence Units'

the police can help you to contact Women's Aid, Social Services or the Housing Department.
• If necessary, transport you (and your children) to a safe place to stay (a refuge or other temporary accommodation).
• Keep good records of all incidents of violence against you.

Police attitudes are slowly changing and, in some parts of Wales, all the above will be done.

Who should charge my partner?

It is misleading for the police to ask you if you want to have your partner charged – it is for the police to decide whether to charge him or not. They may say: 'Do you want to make a complaint?' This means: 'Are you willing to make a statement accusing the man of the assault/incident?' This is because you are the main (and perhaps the only) witness.

They should ask you this out of earshot of your partner. Although you may be frightened, think carefully before you refuse – it is very difficult for the police to proceed if you're not willing to be a witness. If your partner has assaulted you, he has committed a criminal offence and should be charged.

None of this should take place until you are safe. You can ask to speak to a woman police officer if you prefer.

If he's charged, how will that protect me?

If the assault was a serious one, he may be kept in custody until the trial, otherwise he will be released until he appears in court. It may be later the same day or early the next morning. In general, the police do not inform a woman if her partner has been released, but if you phone the police station, they should tell you. It is a condition of police bail that the accused person will not re-offend. You may wish to stay in a Women's Aid refuge until the trial.

However, you will also need to be considering your options for the future as the criminal charges will not be the answer to everything. You may wish to ask the civil courts for an order to protect you in your own home or you may need to move away from the area. You can talk to Women's Aid about your options and see our leaflets.

I'm too frightened to continue, I want to withdraw my statement . . .

Think about why you wish to withdraw your statement – if it's because you've been threatened or you don't have anywhere safe to stay, discuss these problems with Women's Aid or the police – we may find a solution. It is an offence for your partner to threaten you or otherwise try to persuade you to withdraw your support for the prosecution.

The Crown Prosecution Service make the decision whether to pursue the case. They are unlikely to proceed if you are unwilling to be a witness, unless there is other evidence available. However, they can insist on proceeding and if you still refuse to give evidence you could be found guilty of 'contempt of court' in an extreme case.

If I appear in court, my partner will find me!

A friend, relative or Women's Aid worker can accompany you to court to support you. It's a good idea to tell the Clerk of the Court that it is very important to keep your address secret.

What happens in court?

The case will either be heard in a Magistrate's Court or a Crown Court. You are a witness and are therefore not represented by a lawyer. If your partner pleads 'guilty' you will probably not have to give evidence. Often, men change their plea to 'guilty' at the last moment only when it becomes clear that you are not going to withdraw your statement.

What will happen to him if he's found guilty?

The court has a number of options. They can 'bind him over to keep the peace' or 'to be of good behaviour'. This can be in relation to a specific person (i.e. you). He must consent to this and will owe the court a fixed sum of money if he breaks his promise to the court. The 'binding over' lasts for a fixed time period.

Alternatively, he may be fined, placed on probation, have a community service order imposed, or be imprisoned. If he is to be bailed by the court, you can ask your solicitor to discuss the proposed bail conditions with the court clerk or representative of the Crown Prosecution Service with your safety in mind.

What else can I ask the police to do?

If you have fled your home through fear, you may need to return to collect your belongings. You can ask the police to escort you if you are frightened. Ask your local Women's Aid group about this.

In some police forces, there are officers with special responsibility for 'domestic violence'. Some have special units called 'Domestic Violence Units' (or Family Support Units). These may not be at a police station and are usually less formal. Police officers in these units are specially trained and you can discuss the possibilities of pressing criminal charges against your partner with them. They may also be willing to support you through the court procedures.

If I have been injured, is there compensation available?

Yes. You can sue for damages in law – for assault and battery, or for trespass. It is also possible to apply for compensation to the Criminal Injuries Compensation Board. To qualify, there must have been a prosecution and the offender must not benefit from the compensation.

• Please also read Welsh Women's Aid's leaflet: *Do You Need Protection Against Violence?* which explains other ways of using the law. You may also need to seek a solicitor's advice. See page 41 for address details.

© Welsh Women's Aid

Abused women and the law

Information from Scottish Women's Aid

Using a lawyer

A helpful lawyer is a great asset. S/he will be able to explain in more detail the legal rights outlined in this article and describe the court procedures which may be necessary to enforce your rights. If you don't already know a lawyer, your local Women's Aid group or Advice Centre will be able to recommend one for you.

S/he will be able to act on your behalf in applying for housing, or in getting the police to take action against your violent man.

Don't be afraid of going to a lawyer. S/he is there to help you and take your instructions about how you want matters dealt with. Of course you will listen to your lawyer's advice and their professional opinion about your chances of success in any particular course of action. But remember that your lawyer is working for you, not for you and your man as a couple.

If you are unsure about the advice you get from your lawyer, it may be worth checking with an advice agency (such as a Citizens' Advice Bureau) or another lawyer. If you are unhappy with your lawyer, you are entitled to change, even if you have legal aid and/or an action under way. It is better to change sooner rather than later.

Money for legal costs

Do not be put off consulting a lawyer because you are worried about the cost. You may be entitled to financial help towards your legal costs. This help is called Legal Aid, and Legal Advice and Assistance. Your lawyer will help you with filling in the forms.

Some lawyers give a first interview free of charge or charge a small fixed fee – you can find out which ones from your local Citizens' Advice Bureau.

Legal Advice and Assistance

Under this scheme a lawyer can give you advice, write letters, make phone calls, and generally negotiate on your

behalf. S/he can draw up an agreement between yourself and your man, help with housing problems, make an application for you to the Criminal Injuries Compensation Board (see next page), and generally provide advice and assistance on any matter of Scots Law short of going to court for you.

Every lawyer has a 'keycard' which allows them to work out there and then whether you qualify for free legal advice and assistance, or qualify but have to pay a contribution.

If you are on Income Support or Family Credit, you will automatically qualify for free legal advice and assistance. Otherwise your eligibility will depend on your income and capital and the number and ages of your children. If you seek advice because of problems with your husband/partner, his income is disregarded.

If you recover money while being assisted by a lawyer under this scheme, you have to repay your legal costs out of the money you get unless the Legal Aid Board considers that this would cause you financial hardship.

Legal Aid

Under the Legal Aid scheme you can raise court proceedings on the understanding that all, most, or some of your legal costs will be met out of the Legal Aid fund.

In order to qualify you have to satisfy the Legal Aid Board:
1. That you have grounds to raise the action and a reasonable prospect of success, and
2. That you don't have enough income or capital to pay your own legal expenses.

If you are claiming Income Support, you will qualify on financial grounds for Legal Aid but you must still have grounds for the action. If you are not claiming Income Support, the Legal Aid Board will look at all your income and outgoings and decide whether you should get free legal aid or pay a contribution. Most contributions, which rise steeply the more disposable income you have, have to be paid in monthly instalments.

If you need to raise an action urgently, it is possible to have emergency Legal Aid granted immediately. This is done on the understanding that your full application will be successful. If you fail to establish grounds or don't qualify financially or don't co-operate with the Legal Aid Board e.g. by providing information requested, you will receive a bill for the work done by your lawyer while you had an emergency Legal Aid certificate.

If you are awarded a lump sum of more than a certain amount in a divorce action, the Legal Aid Board can make you pay your own expenses out of the balance.

If you have contributions to pay, your lawyer can ask you to pay a sum of money up front, to cover court fees and other charges s/he may have to pay out on your behalf. Before going ahead with any legal action, you should insist on full information from your lawyer.

Appearing in court

Many women worry about taking any kind of legal action because they are afraid of appearing in court. Going to court is likely to be less formal and less frightening than you expect. Ask your lawyer to describe and explain the procedures beforehand. If you can, go to court to hear another case before yours comes up.

Most women who raise an individual (civil) action against their man do not ever have to give evidence in court. Most actions are either not defended, or they start off defended but settle before the stage of a full hearing ('proof'). They are therefore finalised without witnesses having to give evidence at a proof.

In some cases the court will expect affidavits (statements sworn before a lawyer) before granting decrees. These include undefended divorce actions, some custody actions, and applications for an exclusion order.

If you raise an action which is defended and which does not settle, there will usually have to be a proof at which you and your witnesses will have to give evidence.

If your man is charged with a criminal offence (e.g. assaulting you) and he pleads 'not guilty', then you will be called as a witness and will be expected to give evidence in court.

Criminal Injuries Compensation Scheme

If you have been injured as a result of a crime of violence, you can apply for payment of compensation. You have to apply within one year of the date you were injured and your injuries have to be considered to be serious enough.

Other conditions also apply. You must have reported the incident to the police without delay and your man must have been prosecuted (unless there are good reasons why this cannot be done). You cannot apply if you are still living with the man who injured you.

To apply for compensation, you should write to the Criminal Injuries Compensation Authority, Tay House, 300 Bath Street, Glasgow G2 4JR. They will send you a form to fill in and then, after making their own enquiries, they will notify you of their decision. If you are not satisfied with the decision, you can ask for a hearing.

Compensation is usually paid as a lump sum by cheque. Social security payments are deducted in full. If you apply with the help of a lawyer under the Legal Advice and Assistance scheme, you will be expected to pay your own legal costs out of your award unless the Legal Aid Board accepts that this would cause you financial hardship.

• The above is an extract from *Introduction – Abused women and the law*, one of a series of leaflets produced by Scottish Women's Aid.
Other leaflets in the series:
1. *Introduction – Abused women and the law*
2. *Your right to protection from violence in your own home*
3. *Your right to remain in, or return to, your own home*
4. *Your right to put your abusive partner out of your home*
5. *Your right to continuing protection from a violent partner*
6. *Your right to alternative accommodation*
7. *Your right to keep your family home*
8. *Your right to custody of your children*
9. *Your right to a divorce*
10. *Your right to financial help from your partner*

Available from Scottish Women's Aid at 15p each or £3.00 for the pack of ten leaflets with a handy wallet. See page 41 for address details.

Women's Aid provide information, support and safe refuges for abused women and their children if any. You can contact your local Women's Aid group through the phone book, social work department, housing department or police station. Many groups also offer an out-of-office-hours, 24-hours contact number.

© Scottish Women's Aid March, 1999

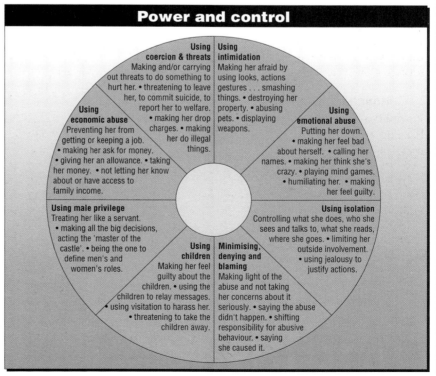

The hidden victims

Children and domestic violence

Recommendations

Domestic violence is known to be a widespread problem affecting families who are wealthy, poor or of average income. This survey and others reveal the guilt and shame caused by domestic violence and mothers' and children's reluctance to reveal it – even where social workers may be aware of a problem. The difficulty in finding a response lies in three areas: ensuring all agencies work together, reinforcing the complexity of the issue and underlining the needs of children.

More help for children living with domestic violence

- All children living in violent situations must be considered to be 'children in need' under the Children Act, and Government must fund local authorities so that they are able to implement these provisions of the Children Act in full.
- Local authorities must ensure that children living with domestic violence are offered appropriate support and help. A range of services are required to meet the varying needs of children of different ages:

1 Visits from social workers to offer advice, assistance and counselling as required.
2 Counselling and play therapy for children who have left violent situations to enable them to overcome the trauma associated with the violence.
3 Counselling for mothers so that they are better able to meet the needs of their children.
4 Family mediation and supervised access arrangements for those situations in which mothers have left violent partners and it is safe and in the interests of children for them to keep in touch with their fathers.
5 Multi-disciplinary support programmes for young people who have grown up in violent situations where there is concern about the effects of their experiences on their behaviour.
6 Top up education programmes to help young people who have lost out on their schooling through domestic violence.

Working together to respond to domestic violence

- Local agencies (education, police, housing, social services, doctors

---

Domestic violence has dramatic short- and longer-term effects on children and their mothers

---

and health visitors) must come together in Domestic Violence Fora to provide a multi-agency response to domestic violence. The needs of children living in violent situations must be at the top of the agenda at such meetings, and services must be available to meet those needs. A key task should be to focus on how the various agencies work together to identify families living with violence and ensure they are offered the help they need. A key responsibility of the Fora should be to provide an advice line for professionals working with children and families. This should provide advice on domestic violence and its impact on children and information on how to respond and get access to the help children may need.

Better support for mothers and children to help them to leave violent situations

- All mothers and children who leave violent situations must have priority access to permanent, affordable housing, without having to spend more than a very short time in temporary accommodation.
- This right should extend to mothers and children who move to a different area to escape domestic violence.

- Government must abandon its plans to amend the homelessness legislation because these mean that mothers and children would lose their right to permanent re-housing.
- Funding for women's refuges must be enhanced and put on a secure footing. Provision should be increased from one family refuge place per 30,000 population to one per 10,000 population.
- Mothers should have priority access to welfare benefits as soon as they have left a violent situation.
- Lone mothers should be offered access to affordable child care and appropriate education and training so that they are able to work to support themselves and their children.

Greater protection for mothers and children suffering violence
- The Law Commission's recommendations must be urgently implemented so that there is a presumption in favour of powers of arrest being attached to injunctions.
- Police protection for women suffering violence must be improved. Enhanced police protection, including the installation of panic buttons, should be offered to those women who have experienced severe or recurrent violence.

Better access for mothers and children to help and advice
- Government should provide for the establishment of a nation-wide, 24-hour domestic violence helpline for women and children. This should be as widely publicised as ChildLine is today.
- Government must ensure that every local authority establishes at least one confidential, community-based support service for mothers and children suffering from domestic violence. Existing family centres may be suitable places in which to base these resources.
- Government must ensure that local authorities publish a range of helpful information leaflets for mothers and children experi-

encing domestic violence and disseminate this widely through doctors' surgeries, schools, libraries etc. Domestic Violence Units should be reviewed and quality standards set.

Heightening the awareness of key professionals
- Police training must be improved so that all police officers, not just those in specialist units, have a better understanding of the impact of domestic violence on children. They must always carry out their overriding duty to protect children and women in violent situations.
- Training and guidance about domestic violence for the judiciary must be improved so that the courts always treat violence against women and children with the seriousness it deserves.
- Education for the key professionals who come into contact with children and mothers (e.g. teachers, social workers, doctors, health visitors) must include better information about the impact of domestic violence and guidance on the appropriate action for them to take for the protection and benefit of children. They should be empowered to alert social services to children living in violent households so that a social worker can visit and appropriate support can be offered.
- Training for professionals

(including police officers, youth workers, probation officers and social workers) who encounter vulnerable young people who are at risk or in trouble must be improved so that they are aware of the possible impact of domestic violence on young people's attitudes and behaviour.

More public education about domestic violence and its effects
- A rolling public education campaign targeted at people living in violent relationships must be launched. It must stress that domestic violence has dramatic short- and longer-term effects on children and their mothers and that such violence is a crime and always the fault of the perpetrator, not the victims.
- The PSHE curriculum in schools should contain material stressing the unacceptability of violence in personal relationships, including some sensitive written material to help those children living with domestic violence.
- Government should reverse its recent decision to allow child-minders to 'smack' children in their care.

• The above is an extract from *The Hidden Victims – Children and Domestic Violence*, produced by NCH Action for Children, ISBN 0 900984 45 7, £5.00, telephone 0345 626579. See page 41 for address details.
© NCH Action for Children

The Women's Aid National Helpline

The Women's Aid National Helpline offers support, help and information to women who are experiencing, or who have experienced, domestic violence. This year over 18,000 women were helped by the Helpline

Who calls the Helpline?

Women experiencing domestic violence	82%
A friend or relative calling on behalf of a woman experiencing domestic violence	4%
Social services, the police, citizens' advice bureaux or other agencies calling on behalf of women experiencing domestic violence	5%
General enquiries about the Helpline service	9%

Types of Helpline calls

Domestic violence – women wanting to talk about their experiences and who are seeking help	34%
Information about emergency accommodation	18%
Information about refuges	10%
Information about legal rights	20%
Information about money, legal aid or welfare benefits	18%

Source: Women's Aid Federation of England

Domestic violence – don't stand for it

Domestic violence is a serious crime. Nobody has the right to abuse you physically, sexually or emotionally. Everyone has the right to live their life free of violence, fear and abuse

If you are in a violent relationship, remember that you are not alone. There are people who can help you.

You may feel frightened, humiliated, alone, ashamed and confused. You are not to blame – if a man assaults his wife or girlfriend, whatever the reason, he is the one with a problem and should recognise it.

There is still a lot of confusion and misunderstanding about domestic violence – what it is, who suffers from it, who commits it and why.

Violence or abuse suffered by women in their home which is carried out by their partner, ex-partner or anyone they are living with is known as domestic violence. Victims of domestic violence are usually women, but this is not always the case.

Women experience domestic violence regardless of their social group, class, age, race, disability, sexuality and lifestyle – it knows no boundaries. Violence and abuse can begin at any time – in the first year or after years of marriage or living together.

Domestic violence can take a number of forms such as physical assault, sexual abuse, rape and threats. In addition, it may include mental and verbal abuse and humiliation. Your partner may not give you any money, constantly criticise you or forbid you to see your friends or family. He may be caring one day and violent the next. He may offer 'rewards' on certain conditions, or in an attempt to persuade you that the abuse won't happen again. However persuasive he may seem, it is likely to get worse over time.

It is not easy to accept that someone you love and have trusted can behave so aggressively towards you. Because they can't explain their partner's behaviour, many women assume that they are to blame.

You have the right to be free of fear and abuse. It is your partner whose behaviour needs to change.

Women experiencing domestic violence tend to play down rather than exaggerate the violence. For some the decision to seek help, to leave the abuser, or get the abuser to leave, is quickly and easily made. For many, the decision will be long and painful as they try to make the relationship work and stop the violence.

Only you can judge your own situation. The groups at the end of this information can offer you help and advice and talk through the various options that are available to you. Women who leave often return to their partners hoping for an improvement in the relationship or because of financial/social pressures.

Never be afraid to ask for help again.

Some women may leave many times before making their final decision.

You should seek legal advice from your local Women's Aid Group, Law Centre, Citizens' Advice Bureau or a solicitor if you are concerned about your children. They can advise you on issues such as parental responsibility, where children should live, with whom they should have contact, changes of school and other related problems.

Despite what their partners say, women do have legal rights in relation to their children. Some men say that if their partner leaves or tells anybody about the violence, their children will be taken away from them. In most cases this will not happen.

Children will react in different ways to being brought up in a home with a violent person.

They may be affected by the tension or by witnessing arguments and assaults. They may feel that they are to blame, or feel insecure, alone, frightened or confused – like you.

Why doesn't she leave?

The graph below sets out the reasons which survey respondents gave for finding it difficult to leave their violent partner for good.

Reason	%
Thought he would change	72%
Afraid of what he might do	63%
Didn't want to leave the home	58%
Didn't want to upset the children	54%
Nowhere to go	49%
Couldn't afford to leave	44%
Too much in love with him	37%
Didn't want to end the relationship	31%
Thought the violence was a 'one off'	23%
Family pressure not to leave	22%

102 respondents

Source: NCH Action for Children 'The Hidden Victims: Children and Domestic Violence';

Talk to them. Be honest with them about the situation they are in. They need to know that the violence is not their fault and that they are not responsible for the way their father/your partner behaves. They should be told that violence is wrong and does not solve problems.

Men who are abusive to women do not necessarily abuse children, but it can happen. If you suspect that this has happened, it is important to talk to them about it and to take steps to protect them (e.g. by seeking advice from social services). Social workers will not take your children away if they can work with you to make sure they are safe.

If you are experiencing violence and abuse in the home, there are three steps you can take:

- the first step is to recognise that it is happening to you and to stop playing down the abuse you are experiencing.
- the second step is to recognise that you are not to blame. No one deserves to be assaulted, humiliated or abused, least of all by their partner in a supposedly caring relationship – there is no excuse.
- the third step is to begin seeking the help and support that is available.

Where to go for support and advice if you are in a violent relationship. If you are being abused by someone, there are organisations that can give you practical and emotional support.

Refuges

Refuges provide safe emergency and temporary accommodation, advice, information, support and a range of other services for women and children escaping violence.

Women's Aid is a key support agency for women and children experiencing domestic violence. The organisation is run by women for women. Women's Aid runs a domestic violence helpline for women experiencing violence and abuse at home. If you need to talk to someone – perhaps for the first time – about the situation you are in, they can offer a sympathetic ear and clear information about housing, legal and other rights.

Their services are confidential and completely free.

- You can contact the Northern Ireland Women's Aid helpline on (01232) 331818

Look in the telephone directory for the telephone number of your local Women's Aid group or local refuge. Social Services, the Samaritans, Housing Executive office and police stations can also give you your Women's Aid local number. Most groups are on call 24 hours a day.

The Samaritans

The Samaritans offer confidential emotional support 24 hours a day by phone, face to face or by letter. There are over 200 branches in the UK and Republic of Ireland staffed by trained volunteers. See your telephone directory for local numbers and addresses or ask the operator who will put you through directly.

The Police

Domestic violence is a crime which the police now deal with as a very serious matter.

They will be sympathetic and provide practical help and information. The RUC has specially trained and experienced officers who will listen and speak to you separately from your partner.

These officers can arrange medical aid, transport and a safe place for you to go. You can ask to speak to a female officer if you wish. Your safety and protection is their priority.

In an emergency dial 999.

Otherwise, you can contact your local police station. They can put you in touch with trained officers who will let you know what other help is available and will offer you support.

Women experience domestic violence regardless of their social group, class, age, race, disability, sexuality and lifestyle – it knows no boundaries

---

Victim Support

Offers information and support to victims of crime. In cases of domestic violence they aim to work closely with Women's Aid. All help given is free and confidential.

You can contact Victim Support direct, or ask the police to put you in contact with your local group.

Health

Many women don't realise the impact their partner's behaviour can have on their health.

They may experience depression and anxiety problems which are often just as severe as any physical ones. This may happen after they have left the relationship because of all the changes and upheavals.

Try to talk about your feelings rather than block them out. If you have to go to casualty try and be open about the cause of your injuries. You can do this in complete confidence.

Talk to your GP or Health Visitor. Tell them the real cause of your worries and injuries. This is vital if they are to give you the proper medical help and support that you need.

Find out if there is a local support group you could go to which could offer you help and counselling.

Your local Social Services Department may also be able to offer you support, particularly if you or your children need care.

Whatever you decide, don't suffer alone. There are lots of people who can help. And don't feel ashamed of what has happened to you – it is not your fault.

Money

One of the reasons that many women stay in an abusive relationship is because they wonder how they will manage financially if they leave.

There are various benefits which you may be able to claim and some can be paid even if you are working. Your local Social Security Office will be able to advise you which benefits you can claim.

Housing

Many women stay in a violent relationship because they feel there is nowhere else to go.

There are several options open to you:

You should contact your local Housing Executive District Office (all telephone numbers are in the telephone book). Your circumstances will be assessed and, if necessary, temporary accommodation can be provided while this happens. It is not likely that you will be deemed to have deliberately made yourself homeless if you have had to leave your home because of violence.

Outside the normal Housing Executive office hours you can use an 'after hours' service should you require temporary accommodation and/or advice. All telephone numbers are at the end of this article.

Other options range from staying with family or friends, renting privately, buying new accommodation or gaining control of your own home.

Domestic violence crisis plan

- Know where the nearest telephone is located.
- Know where refuge can be sought.
- Make a list of important and emergency numbers.
- Save money for bus or taxi fare.
- Have an extra set of keys to home and car.
- Pack an emergency bag – take enough clothes, including school uniforms and children's favourite possessions.
- Consider when it is best to leave. Discuss it with the children. It is important to try to leave with all the children.
- Keep important documents together e.g. benefit books, medical cards, certificates, bank books, legal orders etc.
- Keep a note of the family's essential medicines.

When leaving

- Leave when partner is not around.
- Take all of the children.
- Take personal belongings.
- Take clothing for several days.
- Take toys.
- Take medicine.

Contact point

Women's Aid Helpline: 01232 331818
Samaritans Linkline: 0345 909090
Emergency Services: 999

Northern Ireland Housing Executive

After-hours telephone number for emergencies

South region
(Armagh, West Down and South Down areas)
Newry and Mourne 01693 65511
Armagh/Dungannon 018687 22821
Banbridge/Craigavon 01762 334444

Belfast and South East regions
(Inner Belfast, Greater Belfast, North, Mid and East Down areas):
01232 668246

West region
(Tyrone, Fermanagh and Londonderry areas)
Magherafelt/Cookstown: 01849 468833
Dungannon: 01868 722821
Omagh: 01662 245211
Enniskillen/Fermanagh: 01365 324711
Londonderry/Limavady/Strabane: 01504 45171

North East region
(Co Antrim and East Londonderry areas)
Antrim: 01849 468833

Remember

- Domestic violence is a serious crime.
- Everyone has the right to live their life free of fear, threats and abuse.
- If you are a victim you are not alone; there are people who can help you.
- Your partner's violence is not your fault.
- Contact Women's Aid and/or the police for further help and advice.

© Northern Ireland Women's Aid Federation

Domestic violence in Northern Ireland

The recent rise in recorded incidents of domestic violence by many agencies, particularly since the ceasefires, needs close analysis.

We can offer several explanations. Police training has greatly improved their response and recording of statistics and many more referrals are coming to the Helpline from that quarter.

While simplistic links between the troubles and domestic violence are unhelpful, it has to be acknowledged that thirty years of violent conflict in the civil and political arena is reflected in the whole of society. Families live within a social context and research evidence supports the view that, in conflict and war situations, domestic violence escalates, the problems are compounded and there is a higher incidence.

The attitudes which underlie civil and sectarian conflicts are the same as those which give rise to violence and abuse in the home.

Domination, control, coercion, and inability to value and celebrate differences, these are the hallmarks of perpetrators of violence in every sphere of life.

We are either part of the solution or part of the problem, none of us can be neutral. Coalitions against domestic violence in the United States recognise that effective prevention strategies will also prevent gang violence, youth violence, elder abuse etc. Here, we might add sectarian violence and political violence.

© Northern Ireland Women's Aid Federation

Women's Aid in Scotland

What is Women's Aid in Scotland?

We are an all-woman network of 38 (April 1999) affiliated local Women's Aid groups and their national office. We are a confidential organisation which provides information, support and safe refuge for women, children and young people who are experiencing or have experienced domestic abuse.

What is domestic abuse?

Domestic abuse is the physical, mental and/or sexual abuse of a woman by someone with whom she is or has been in a relationship.

Physical abuse can include slapping, punching, strangling, using weapons, scalding, burning.

Mental abuse can include humiliation and degradation, threats against the woman or her children, name-calling.

Sexual abuse can include being forced to take part in sex acts against her will, being sexually assaulted with objects, being raped.

Witnessing the abuse of their mother is emotional abuse of children and there are links between domestic abuse and all forms of child abuse.

Who experiences domestic abuse?

Any woman can be abused, there is no 'typical abused woman'. It is likely that we all know women who have been abused. In Women's Aid, we see women from all backgrounds, all ages, all sections of society.

Children and young people also experience domestic abuse, either by seeing or hearing their mother's abuse, or by being abused themselves.

Is domestic abuse a widespread problem?

Research shows that 1 in 4 women experience abuse at some time in their lives. In Scotland, Women's Aid groups receive over 50,000 requests for help every year.

What can Women's Aid do?

- We can offer information and support through our offices, many of which provide an out of office hours service. We can tell a woman, or someone contacting us on her behalf, about her legal rights, housing options and entitlement to benefits. We can provide an opportunity to talk to someone about what has been happening.
- We can provide accommodation in our safe refuges, houses at secret addresses around Scotland. Women on their own or with their children and young people, can stay in our refuges as long as they need to. There are also refuges in the rest of Britain, so women can move out of their own area to be safe. We have two refuges for black women and children, if they wish to use this option, and some provision is available for disabled women and children.
- We provide services for children and young people as well as their mothers. Children's support work includes individual work, group work and play. This enables children to talk about their experiences, make sense of their fears and worries, gain mutual support, improve self-esteem and feel happier.

How is Women's Aid funded?

We are a charitable organisation and rely on fundraising and the support of the community. The national office receives partial funding from the Scottish Office and local groups receive grants from their local authority.

How we can help you

- Provide leaflets, posters
- Provide training and consultation tailored to your organisation's needs
- Provide speakers for conferences and seminars
- Provide information about domestic abuse
- Provide support to help set up new groups

How you can help us

- Tell women, children and young people about Women's Aid
- Give a donation – we need to fundraise to survive
- Challenge attitudes – no one deserves to be abused
- Display our posters and leaflets
- Ask us to provide training in your workplace
- Support your local Women's Aid group

© Scottish Women's Aid

Both sexes equally likely to suffer domestic violence

Men are increasingly the victims of domestic violence, and are just as likely as women to be assaulted by a partner, according to Home Office research published yesterday.

The men most likely to be attacked are in their early 30s and unmarried, but living with a woman.

The findings, from the British Crime Survey, show there are some 6.6 million incidents of assault in the home each year, evenly split between men and women.

But the research also shows that women are twice as likely to be injured, and are much more likely to suffer repeated attacks. They are also less likely to be in a financial position to be able to leave a violent relationship.

It also shows that the rise in domestic attacks on men by women is a 1990s' phenomenon. In 1995 just over 4 per cent of men and women said they had been assaulted by a current or former partner in the last year. But 23 per cent of women said they had been assaulted by a partner at some time – compared with 15 per cent of men.

Women are at greatest risk of attack after a relationship has broken up or they and their spouse have separated. The researchers say women have a different emotional reaction to separation, and are less

*By Alan Travis,
Home Affairs Editor*

likely to use violence to express their feelings: 'Women's violence against men is, therefore, more likely to be within the context of a relationship.'

> *Findings from the British Crime Survey show there are some 6.6 million incidents of assault in the home each year, evenly split between men and women*

The research was published as the Home Office Minister Paul Boateng and the Leader of the Lords, Baroness Jay, launched *Break the Chain*, a domestic violence leaflet giving practical advice and listing telephone helplines, including a men's advice line.

'Domestic violence wrecks lives. Much of it is literally criminal,' said Mr Boateng. 'All of it is unacceptable. But a basic shift in attitudes is

required. We must work towards the day when such conduct is universally recognised as reprehensible.'

The study by Home Office researchers Catriona Mirrlees-Black and Carole Byron found that in most cases the violence involved pushing and grabbing, but in 47 per cent of incidents the victim was also kicked, slapped or punched. About half the attacks resulted in injury, most commonly bruising, but one in 10 involved cuts and a small minority broken bones.

Throwing things at each other happens in one in five cases, and in about a third of cases children in the home either witnessed the attack or were aware of it.

Only half of victims of domestic assault told anyone about it – normally a friend, neighbour or relative. The police were only told about 12 per cent of incidents.

For men and women, East Anglia has the highest level of domestic assault followed by the North and Yorkshire/Humberside. Assaults are below average in London and the South-east, and women in the East Midlands and men in Wales are at the lowest risk.

• *Domestic Violence*: Home Office Research Study 191; HMSO

*© The Guardian
January, 1999*

ADDITIONAL RESOURCES

You might like to contact the following organisations for further information. Due to the increasing cost of postage, many organisations cannot respond to enquiries unless they receive a stamped, addressed envelope.

Barnardo's
Tanners Lane
Barkingside
Ilford, Essex, IG6 1QG
Tel: 0181 550 8822
Fax: 0181 551 6870
Web site: www.barnardos.org.uk
Works to help each person to achieve his or her potential. Produces factsheets on domestic violence issues specific to children's services.

ChildLine
2nd Floor Royal Mail Building
Studd Street
London, N1 0QW
Tel: 0171 239 1000
Fax: 0171 239 1001
Web site: www.childline.org.uk
ChildLine is free, national helpline for children and young people in trouble or danger. Children or young people can phone or write free of charge about problems of any kind to: ChildLine, Freepost 1111, London N1 0BR, Tel: Freephone 0800 1111. Has produced *It Hurts me Too*, a joint publication with the Women's Aid Federation of England.

NCH Action for Children
85 Highbury Park
London, N5 1UD
Tel: 0171 226 2033
Fax: 0171 226 2537
Web site: www.ncafc.org.uk
Has produced two publications looking at children and domestic violence: *The Hidden Victims* and *Making a Difference*, both priced at £5.00 and available from the NCH Hotline on 0345 626579.

Northern Ireland Women's Aid Federation
129 University Street
Belfast, BT7 1HP
Tel: 01232 249041
Fax: 01232 239296
E-mail: niwaf@dnet.co.uk
The aims of The Northern Ireland Women's Aid Federation (NIWAF) are – the provision of refuge and ongoing support to women and their children suffering abuse within the home; to encourage a process of self-help and recognition of the emotional needs of children involved in domestic violence.

NSPCC – National Society for the Prevention of Cruelty to Children
National Centre
42 Curtain Road
London, EC2A 3NH
Web site: www.nspcc.org.uk
Tel: 0171 825 2500
Fax: 0171 825 2525
Has a network of Child Protection Teams and projects to protect children from abuse. Can help parents, carers and relatives who feel they may be in danger of harming their children. Operates the Child Protection Helpline offering counselling and support Tel: 0800 800 500.

Refuge
2-8 Maltravers Street
London, WC2R 3EE
Tel: 0171 395 7700
Fax: 0171 395 7721
Refuge provides accommodation and a unique range of professional, high-quality services for over 650 abused women and children each year. If you are a woman needing advice or help call their 24-hour National Crisis Line on 0990 995443. Produces publications about the work of Refuge and facts about domestic violence.

Scottish Women's Aid
Norton Park
57 Albion Road
Edinburgh, EH7 5QY
Tel: 0131 475 2372
Fax: 0131 475 2384
Scottish Women's Aid is a confidential organisation which provides information, support and safe refuge for women, children and young people who are experiencing or have experienced domestic abuse. Produces leaflets on domestic violence, the law, parental rights and responsibilities and young people's rights.

Victim Support
Cranmer House
39 Brixton Road
London, SW9 6DZ
Tel: 0171 735 9166
Fax: 0171 582 5712
Victim Support's work with domestic violence focuses on female victims of domestic violence. This focus does not mean that we deny the existence of other forms of relationship violence, but the focus of Victim Support's work is on services for women because statistics and experience show that the majority of cases fall into this category. Victim Supportline 0845 30 30 900, Mon-Fri 9am-9pm, Sat/Sun 9am-7pm.

Welsh Women's Aid
38-48 Crwys Road
Cardiff, CF2 4NN0
Tel: 01222 390874
Fax: 01222 390878
Welsh Women's Aid is the national network of local Women's Aid groups in Wales. Produces leaflets; ask for their publications list.

Women's Aid Federation of England (WAFE)
PO Box 391
Bristol, BS99 7WS
Tel: 0117 944 4411
Fax: 0117 924 1703
E-mail: wafe@wafe.co.uk
Provides advice, information and temporary refuge for women and their children who are threatened by mental, emotional or physical violence, harassment, or sexual abuse. Runs the Women's Aid National Helpline: 0345 023 468. Mon-Thurs 10am-5pm; Fri 10am-3pm. Produces leaflets and books, including 6 very good leaflets at 10p. Ask for their publications list.

INDEX

The Internet has been likened to shopping in a supermarket without aisles. The press of a button on a Web browser can bring up thousands of sites but working your way through them to find what you want can involve long and frustrating on-line searches. And unfortunately many sites contain inaccurate, misleading or heavily biased information. Our researchers have therefore undertaken an extensive analysis to bring you a selection of quality Web site addresses.

* * * * *

Family Violence Awareness Page
http://www.famvi.com
This US-based site is devoted to helping fight all forms of family violence and to providing information about services available to families that are in need of assistance. You will also find links to other sites. In addition, there are articles, essays and readers' comments.

The Family Violence Prevention Fund (FUND)
http://www.igc.apc.org/fund
The Family Violence Prevention Fund (FUND) is a national non-profit organisation that focuses on domestic violence education, prevention and public policy reform. This site contains information on men and domestic violence and useful tips on mobilising a campaign against violence. A section on women's personal stories of victimisation and survival takes one beyond the statistics to the real picture.

Violence Against Women Office (US)
http://www.usdoj.gov/vawo
This extensive US Department of Justice site provides information on state, regional, and national resources, links to police departments with domestic violence pages, factsheets, and many other links. It also includes a plethora of government information on domestic violence including legislation, reports and studies, speeches and press releases.

Men and Women Against Domestic Violence
www.silcom.com/~paladin/madv
Men and Women Against Domestic Violence is an internet-based coalition of men and women working to address the issue of domestic violence. They declare that this is not just a women's issue, but is very much a men's issue, too. Also provides links to other domestic violence internet resources.

SafetyNet: US Domestic Violence Resources
http://home.cybergrrl.com/dv
A little dated now but this site offers a wide range of resources, statistics and other information regarding domestic violence in the US.

Women's Aid Federation of England (WAFE)
www.womensaid.org.uk
Women's Aid is the key national charity in England for women and children experiencing physical, sexual or emotional abuse in their homes. Their site offers information if you need help with the following: women experiencing domestic violence, finding a safe place to stay, local refuge telephone numbers, information about domestic violence, Women's Aid services, publications, briefing papers, training and other services, contact numbers and addresses, information on Women's Aid membership, facts and figures, basic domestic violence research findings and useful web sites including refuges.

ACKNOWLEDGEMENTS

The publisher is grateful for permission to reproduce the following material.

While every care has been taken to trace and acknowledge copyright, the publisher tenders its apology for any accidental infringement or where copyright has proved untraceable. The publisher would be pleased to come to a suitable arrangement in any such case with the rightful owner.

Chapter One: Domestic Violence

The context of domestic violence, © NCH Action for Children, *Quarter of women face violence in the home*, © Telegraph Group Limited, London 1998, *GPs to monitor home violence*, © The Independent, November 1998, *Domestic violence*, © South Glamorgan County Council, *Domestic violence – the myths*, © Women's Aid Federation of England (WAFE), *Domestic violence – facts*, © Women's Aid Federation of England (WAFE), *Why do we love men who beat us?*, © The Daily Mail, January 1998, *The difficulty of leaving for good*, © NCH Action for Children, *Lucy's story*, © Refuge, *Violent husbands face a ban from seeing the children*, © The Daily Mail, June 1999, *At last, help for women living in fear*, © The Independent, July, 1999, © The Daily Mail, January 1998, *Factors which persuaded mothers to finally leave their violent partners*, © NCH Action for Children, *What had I done?*, © The Daily Mail, April 1998, *How many seek refuge?*, © Women's Aid Federation of England (WAFE), *Crackdown on domestic violence*, © The Guardian, November 1998, *Domestic violence*, © Barnardo's, June 1998, *The cruel truth about the way the courts treat kids*, © The Independent, April 1999, *Domestic violence: a rural and urban crime*, © Victim Support, Autumn 1998, *Violence against women*, © World Health Organisation (WHO)/OMS, 1998.

Chapter Two: Seeking Help

Domestic violence – who can help?, © Women's Aid Federation of England (WAFE), *The difficulty mothers and children faced in finding somewhere to go when they left violent situations*, © NCH Action for Children, *Stop the violence*, © NSPCC, *Protecting children from family violence*, © NSPCC, June 1999, *The end of the line*, © Refuge, *There is a hiding place*, © The Express, December 1998, *What can I expect from the police?*, © Welsh Women's Aid, *Abused women and the law*, © Scottish Women's Aid, *The hidden victims*, © NCH Action for Children, *The Women's Aid National Helpline*, © Women's Aid Federation of England (WAFE), *Domestic violence – don't stand for it*, © Northern Ireland Women's Aid Federation, *Why doesn't she leave?*, © NCH Action for Children, *Domestic violence in Northern Ireland*, © Northern Ireland Women's Aid, *Women's Aid in Scotland*, © Scottish Women's Aid, *Both sexes equally likely to suffer domestic violence*, © The Guardian, January 1999.

Photographs and illustrations:

Pages 1, 4, 18, 22, 29, 32, 39: Pumpkin House, pages 6, 15, 20, 24, 31, 34, 40: Simon Kneebone, page 9: Andrew Smith.

Craig Donnellan
Cambridge
September, 1999